The Curious History of Love

The Curious
History of Love

———————

Jean-Claude Kaufmann

by David Macey

polity

First published in French as *L'étrange histoire de l'amour heureux* © Armand Colin, 2009

This English edition © Polity Press, 2011

Polity Press
65 Bridge Street
Cambridge CB2 1UR, UK

Polity Press
350 Main Street
Malden, MA 02148, USA

ISBN-13: 978-0-7456-5153-8
ISBN-13: 978-0-7456-5154-5(pb)

A catalogue record for this book is available from the British Library.

Typeset in 11 on 13 pt Sabon
by Toppan Best-set Premedia Limited
Printed and bound in Great Britain by the MPG Books Group

The publisher has used its best endeavours to ensure that the URLs for external websites referred to in this book are correct and active at the time of going to press. However, the publisher has no responsibility for the websites and can make no guarantee that a site will remain live or that the content is or will remain appropriate.

Every effort has been made to trace all copyright holders, but if any have been inadvertently overlooked the publisher will be pleased to include any necessary credits in any subsequent reprint or edition.

For further information on Polity, visit our website: www.politybooks.com

Contents

Monsieur Kaufmann

I am writing you this letter because I was very moved by your article 'The Economic Mistake' in <u>Psychologies Magazine</u>. I completely agree with you: there really is something we don't understand, and something is wrong with our modern world. The accumulation of wealth and facile consumerism are nothing more than screens that cover up a great psychological poverty. And intellectual poverty. It would be so nice to discover a storehouse of knowledge instead of all this media fuss about scraps of information that don't help us to understand anything. So I was very intrigued by the strange tale you tell about how a vision of the individual was invented, about how nothing was pre-ordained and about how it could all have been very different. I underlined this passage: 'Society has come to be centred on the economy, and the economy has come to be centred on an incredibly false and reductive vision of what human beings are. It is a hateful vision (the calculating individual is inevitably selfish). And it is a false vision because human beings do have feelings and are eager to give their lives a wider meaning.'

That's fascinating, and I agree completely. But your one failing is that you never offer any solution. That's fine. Perhaps you don't want to write self-help manuals, but you might at least show some commitment and tell us how we can replace that reductive vision with something else. Everyone knows that it can't last much longer and that the crisis we are going through is just a foretaste of things to come.

Personally, I think that the 'something else' has to be love. Why not make love the centre of society, why not live on hugs and kindness (and sex, for those who like that sort of thing)? I don't understand why we didn't try to base society upon love a long time ago. And then I say to myself that someone must have tried, and that it didn't work. I'm thinking of the communities of May '68, which did not last long. I'd like to know more about all that. And while we're on the subject, I'd quite simply like to know how love works. I'm talking to the sociologist here, because I have the impression that scientists haven't dealt with this question directly. Apart from the biologists, who are all the rage these days. But they tell us that it's all to do with hormones. If only it were that simple! In their world, feelings become molecules, and that is as depressing as the world of the economists. No, what I'd like to know is how this happened in social terms (perhaps I should say 'in political terms' - I'm not too sure about that). Have there ever been societies that were centred on love, and how did they work out? It seems to me that, if we take that as our starting point, we might find out if it is possible to build a society on love, and how to set about building it.

I also have the feeling that this might provide us with some more personal clues as to how love works. We don't really know how it works any more. I don't want to tell you my life story, because that is not what this letter is about, but, like a lot of other women, I've had my share of disappointments. I was in a really miserable relationship, and I didn't even have the courage to get out of it and then one day he traded me in for a younger model. Bitch! I was so stunned that it took away all the pleasure of being a free woman again. I really liked your book <u>The Single Woman and the Fairy-Tale Prince</u> (Kaufmann 2008a [2006]) and it was a great help at the time. But it didn't give me any answers about the future. And now I'm very frightened about committing myself again. And the worst thing of all is that I'm so frightened of being swept off my feet in emotional terms even though I can fall in love at the drop of a hat. I suppose that's the contradiction I have to live with: I dream of a society based upon love, but in personal terms I keep my emotions in check because I'm afraid I'll be let down if I fall in love again. Help me, doctor!

With my best wishes
Isolde

Dear Isolde,

Thank you for your letter. An old-fashioned letter, hand-written and sent through the post. No name, no address, just your signature. 'Isolde' is obviously not your real name (no one is called Isolde these days) but as you will see, you could not have chosen a better pseudonym because we will be talking about Tristan later. You obviously don't expect an answer, and that's fine by me. I've had so much to say about love for so long, but I've never found a way to do it. I was frightened. Frightened of lapsing into boring academic clichés, which are the last thing we need in this domain, and frightened of looking intolerably pretentious (who can claim to tell the truth about love?). And frightened of being told: 'Just leave us alone with our passions and don't bother us with your academic twaddle!'

Your letter provides me with the opportunity I was waiting for, and gives me an excuse. So I'll make the most of it. Because I don't even know whether you will read this book, even though I wrote it with you in mind. It takes the form of a letter, an answer to your questions. The epistolary form allowed me to find the lightness of touch that we need when we are talking about a subject that is both very dense in historical terms and fiendishly complex. There is nothing simple about love.

Introduction

Everything to do with Love is a mystery:
His arrows, his quiver, his torch and his childhood.
Exhausting this science is not
Something that can be done in a day:
So I make no claim to explain everything here
                          Jean de la Fontaine, *L'Amour et la folie*

Your letter raises a lot of questions. Yes, there is a growing feeling that something is not right: modern society is cold, cruel and full of injustice, and it cannot make us happy. It satisfies our material needs almost too easily, but it is emotionally dead. All this could have been completely different if history had taken a different direction and if love had been able to establish itself as a political principle. Unfortunately, that did not happen. You ask me if anyone ever thought of building a society based on love, and consisting of caresses and kindness. The answer is 'yes'. In fact many people have tried to do so. Love dreamed of ruling the world for centuries. It failed. You are right when you say that scientists have not paid enough attention to analysing the feeling of love. The history of love's political failures, in particular, has yet to be written. And yet that history is essential if we wish to understand how we reached this point, and if we wish to know whether we still stand some chance of introducing more gentleness and altruism into the management of human affairs.

You ask me – 'quite simply' – how love works. I think that it is impossible to explain that in any detail without retracing the whole history that has made love what it is today. The keys to understanding its history, and the more personal themes that you evoke, are to be found in a past of which we know little. A few behavioural rules are really not enough. Before we imagine how we could make better use of it today, in both social and individual terms, we have to understand where love comes from by understanding its surprising battles, its victories and defeats.

OF LOVE

Love! It is impossible to say or write the word without feeling some emotion. Our lips do not say 'love' in the way that they say other words. The very word evokes hundreds and hundreds of years of impulses, caresses and dreams. Irrepressible desires and sublime passions. So it is difficult to adopt the detached stance of the cold scientist when we are talking about love. Stendhal learned that to his cost. He wanted to write a treatise that could accurately analyse the mechanisms of this precious feeling. Sadly, his categories and classifications struggled to say what three pages of one of his novels can convey so easily. Fortunately, there is more than that to *Love* (Stendhal 1975 [1822]). Many passages actually tell us about Stendhal's own infatuation with the passionate Carbonora Métilde (Crouzet 1965). But we will come back to Stendhal in a moment, as he intervenes in a key episode in the story I will be telling.

Given that I have mentioned Stendhal, I ought to say a word about the novelists and poets. They have bequeathed us so much literature on love that they are a real problem for the poor researcher. (Has so much been written about any other theme?) How can we sort out what is and what is not acceptable from the scientific point of view? Should we even try to? Or should we try to put it into perspective, and try to explain how this type of literature came into existence, and what role it plays? That is what I have decided to do. Literature is not a distorted reflection of the reality of love: it tells us what forms love will take in future, and it lies at the heart of the social factory where feelings are made.

The social factory? Yes, I know: the word 'love' suggests something personal and intimate. Indeed, nothing could be more personal and intimate, and that is what proves that it is a genuine feeling: 'Listen to what your heart tells you.' And love is right to evoke the heart because it is a profoundly emotional and subjective experience. We are all familiar with that side of love. But that is not what we will be talking about here. There is a very different side to the history of love.

If we take lived experience as a starting point, the history of love appears to be stable and straightforward. Some of the questions that have been asked about love for hundreds, if not thousands, of years even seem to suggest that it is a feeling that never changes, that has always existed, with only a few variations, in all societies. And yet nothing could be less like a peaceful river than the love factory (which produces the language of love, the ways of making love and the forms of feeling that any given society knows at any given period (Luhmann 1990 [1982])). On the contrary, it is the setting for bitter struggles between rival visions and for many an upheaval. And that, of course, is enough to provide the plot for my story. Take, for example, the curious fact that the dominant form of contemporary love – the quiet longing to be happy – is a direct descendant of the most tragic episodes of earlier eras. Anthony Giddens (1992) is right to say that love-as-passion has always existed, but that romanticism is a very special form of love that has left its mark on one moment in our history. But he ought to have added that the passions were never the same after romanticism. A major event had taken place, and it changed everyone's experience of love for ever.

Should we be talking about love or 'loves'? There are so many kinds of love that one wonders whether we can really talk about it in the singular – especially in languages like French or English, in which we can use the same word to say that 'I love' my wife, my car or my dog. What is the common factor between the passionate love we feel for one person, and the one, universal love we feel for other people in general; between the most animal physical desire, and the must sublime mystical passions? 'Depending on whether we are feeling gloomy or cheerful, timid or sensual or voluptuous, the common factor appears to be sorrow or pleasure, languor or frenzy, constancy or lies, lust or purity' (Planhol 1921: 5). And yet, René de Planhol goes on, 'all these things really are aspects of love, either in turn or all at once. Love contains all these feelings.' Separating out all these different contents (passionate love, parental tenderness, human generosity, holy adoration . . .) certainly gives us an overview of what is going on. But it does not help us to understand what love really is, where it comes from or what hides behind its sudden and incomprehensible mood swings. The mystery, if there is one, lies in the fact that in it very different extremes are intimately bound up with one another, and that the heart of love is to be found in its contradictory dynamics. That explains, for example, how the blackest of tragedies could give birth to a gentle happiness.

The actual experience of love obviously knows nothing of these contradictions. It is precisely because it seems so simple that it feels so complete. Whatever form it takes, and whatever its content – and it can be either passionate or simply generous – it take us out of ourselves (out of the narrow, egotistical circle of the old self), attracts us to someone else, and makes us become attached to someone else. It creates something of a social bond, and it does so in the most intimate and sensual way. And because it all happens so quickly, we think that love is a sort of feeling that exists outside time, that it is a strictly personal adventure that takes place far away from society and its quarrels and debates. But it would be nothing without those quarrels and debates. We forget the extent to which, before they became minor personal issues, love and the passions were themes that were widely debated in the hope of changing the world. The journey on which we are about to embark may seem surprising because some of the lands we will be travelling through (the esoteric sophistication of religious thought and the violence of political struggles) look very unfamiliar. And yet we have to make that detour if we wish to understand what lies behind today's emotions. When someone whispers 'I love you' or when we feel their gentle touch, we sense this history, and that is what gives the words and gestures their specific form. We have to plunge into this distant past if we are to be able to answer the most concrete questions we are now asking ourselves.

The times we live in! They are cruel, and they are hard and uncaring. Life is an ordeal for the individual. The greatest capacities of the human mind are now being mobilized in an attempt to understand very minor technical issues (economic models) that are of no great interest in themselves. They are of no great interest either in terms of morality of knowledge, or in terms of any of the things that give life its grandeur and its savour. Is this real life? Of course it is not. Real life is obviously elsewhere, in the search for what it is that makes humanity human, in all that is best about the way we feel. Don't let the veneer of fashionable cynicism fool you: our desire for love is boundless. But as every episode in my history teaches us, desire is not, unfortunately, enough.

History is a science whose very name suggests the idea of a narrative plot. History and story originally meant the same thing: we wrote history by telling stories. And I would like the story I am telling to unfold in the same way. I may simplify things at times, and I will give my own interpretations a free rein (but I will, I believe, remain true to the essential facts), and I hope that the historians will forgive me.

DRAMATIS PERSONAE

The favourite theme of the light comedy known in France as *théâtre de boulevard* is the classic schema of a clash between three characters (wife, husband, lover). Whilst there is nothing comic about the story I am about to tell, it too revolves mainly around three main characters. It seemed to me that it would be useful to introduce them briefly.

Our first two characters represent very different forms of love. Love obviously takes more than two forms: it is multifaceted and constantly changes. Yet despite all the variations, we can identify two essential forms. They are very different, and they are often rivals.

Our first character is the love that aspires to being universal, all-encompassing and systematic. It takes little heed of the specific qualities of the one it loves because the main thing is to go on loving for ever, and to love everyone. It wants to transcend its actual partner and to become a love that nothing can shake. It wants to subvert the planet with its generosity and self-sacrifice. This love has been heavily influenced by the Christian tradition ('Love thine enemy as thyself'), which has given it the name *agape*.

We also find it in the secular configuration of political utopias that are based upon the principle of mutual benevolence. And, in a more private form, in the internal solidarities that bind together families.

This form of love has two basic characteristics. Whilst it aspires to being universal, it is deeply rooted in reality, and accepts reality's limitations or shortcomings, even though it would prefer to overlook them. It is based upon a wisdom and an art and uses a loving gaze to metamorphose everything that the accidents of life throw up.

The second form of love is almost its complete antithesis. We are talking about passion, and there is nothing universal about passion. On the contrary, it singularizes everything. Its love-object is the only thing that matters, and everything else becomes invisible and of no importance. The real world loses its savour, and is of no interest. Passion takes us into a different world. This is a world that only those who are in love know about. Its dreams and feelings are so strong that it makes them forget all about ordinary life. Whereas *agape* actually loves what is ordinary, passion rejects it in the name of a more exciting ideal. And whereas *agape* is a tranquil wisdom, there is nothing tranquil about passion. It takes a lot of emotional intensity to wrest lovers away from the old world.

These two forms of love are not just variations on one another, and we cannot simply add them together. They are completely different, and any display of one weakens the other and vice versa. And that is, as it happens, one of the underlying reasons why love has never succeeded in ruling the world. The permanent confrontation between these two forms of love also allows our third character to make his entrance and – inevitably – to become the star of the show.

Our third character is very different, and is anti-love personified. It is cold and egotistic. How could such a hateful figure come to play the starring role? The story I am about to tell will explain that. For the moment, let us just say that, to begin with, it looks like something much more attractive. Reason outlined an enlightened programme that would allow us to understand society, and it associated its programme with a mutual benevolence. Unfortunately, it proved to be just as incapable of controlling the affairs of the world as love was. And so, Reason was reduced to being nothing more than a minor technique: self-interested calculation. Everything that is noble about Reason was swept away, and all that remained was mean and despicable, namely cold calculation and selfish competition. Stripped of its more generous attributes, what should have been an economic model for the individual became a fearfully effective way of managing society. For better or for worse. Love had been defeated.

SYNOPSIS

Our story begins long before our third character comes on stage. In ancient societies, thoughts and behaviours were governed by a system of shared values. There were many debates about the role that love should play, and about how it could become a form of government. I refer, of course, to the first form of love, which promoted a universal empathy, and whose social virtues were praised because it brought people together. At this time, passion had a very bad reputation. It took the form of anarchic eruptions that were stimulated by physical desire, and it posed a threat to the social order.

All this began to change in about the twelfth century, when passion suddenly began to look very different. It was no longer pure instinctual anarchy, and it now had a project of its own. It was, it has to be said, a very strange project that had emerged from the esoteric depths of hundreds and hundreds of years of thinking on the part of religious sects that were both marginal and extremist. It was also unrealistic, but it underwent a strange reversal: its public failure gave rise to new ways of behaving and thinking in our private lives. Many of our words and gestures still show its influence. The same process was repeated several times: the changes that occurred within the private realm and that strengthened it made up for all love's political failures. The gloom of a political project that could not be realized in this world gave way to the joyful colours of new love rituals.

Everything changed in about the twelfth century as individuals gradually shook off the yoke of society and tried to define their own values. Passion offered an alternative to the weight of tradition and the interference of the family. At this point, there was a moment of intense competition and conflict between the two forms of love. Our third character immediately took advantage of this, and took the stage. He was discreet to begin with. He modestly offered to be of service, and to keep the social peace. He rejected the idea that passion might be a model for individual emancipation: all passion did was stir up unstable moods, and it might lead to all kinds of dreadful excesses. A sense of where one's interests lay and rational calculations also offered a model for individual emancipation and, our third character insisted, made it possible to put human relationships on a much more stable footing. We will go into this in more detail in Chapter 2, which tells the sad story of how the model of the selfish and calculating individual became central to the workings of society.

The tragedy is that, once this model had become central, it was impossible to displace it, and its hold became stronger and stronger. Vaguely aware that they had been caught in a trap, love's revolutionaries rebelled and tried to invent a different world. Some had no hesitation about taking up arms, whilst others peacefully dreamed up grandiose utopias. Romanticism finally gave passion a new lease of life. Chapter 3 will describe these magnificent, desperate attempts, which so often, sadly, ended in failure. But these political failures produced some remarkable innovations in the private realm. Romanticism, in particular, created a way of thinking that still has a more powerful influence on us than we might think.

The history of love takes place on two different levels. There are lots of fights in the factory where categories or representations are manufactured, and reversals of fortune are common. The evolution of behaviours, on the other hand, is much steadier. It is influenced by struggles over the definition of love, but it records them slowly, overcoming contradictions and smoothing out all the wrinkles. Chapter 4 describes how today's loving couple gradually came into being.

The final chapter looks at the contemporary situation, which is both tragic and wonderful. It is tragic because the 'calculating individual' model has become so powerful that it is now encroaching upon the private realm. Our choice of conjugal partner, in particular, is increasingly influenced by a consumerist logic (comparing products in order to find out which is best), and that makes commitment very problematic. And it is wonderful because, paradoxically enough, the woes of the world put us under an obligation to be happy. The more the cold cynicism of the calculating individual becomes central to the system, the more we want to find happiness – in purpose-built spaces where, thanks to love, we can find some consolation. As the centre of society becomes increasingly harsh and cold, we aspire to finding the happy love that will heal all our wounds.

That aspiration is so strong that it has a truly revolutionary import. Surely the desire for a happy love can subvert the system by gnawing away at its edges. Although we are not always aware of it, a pitiless struggle is going on between two models of love. This is why we experience so many changes of heart in our personal lives; at times, we are coldly calculating, and then, a few moments later, we sacrifice ourselves without a second thought. The new art consists in knowing which attitude to adopt without being too calculating, as that would turn our hearts to stone.

I have said too much about love in the singular in this brief synopsis. In their desire to overcome the selfish individual, *agape* and passion – which have both been converted to the search for happiness – are now trying to form an alliance. But the differences between them are too great. Their differences are rooted in their long and conflicting histories. Like its forebears, today's conjugal *agape* wants to be part of ordinary life. Passion, in contrast, still dreams of escaping it. Although the plot has undergone some changes, the main three characters in my little play are still the same. The strange story of love is not over yet.

1

Where Does Love Come From?

In an ideal world, a story should have a clearly defined beginning – which means that I have a problem from the outset. Love has always existed in all societies. At times, it coexisted alongside an *ars erotica* that was so sophisticated as to make us jealous. At other times it coexisted alongside a poetic art (Paz 1995 [1994]) or a sentimental art. In *Tristes Tropiques*, Claude-Lévi Strauss (1974 [1955]) explains why the erotic atmosphere that permeated the day-to-day life of the Nambikwaras made such an impression on him. Sensuality was everywhere but it was sublimated by a playful and sensual quest. One could give countless other examples drawn from the most disparate cultures. One thinks, for instance, of the sophisticated ethics of India's *Kama Sutra*, or of pre-Confucian China, where sexuality was seen as the most natural thing in the world (Gulik 1961). In the Egypt of the Pharaohs, the copulating gods symbolized the rebirth of nature in springtime (Lambert 2007). Fertility and procreation have almost always been bound up with the sacred. There were countless phallic rituals in which emblems of erect penises were brandished as though they were so many promises. And there were countless ceremonies celebrating the pleasures that are associated with procreation. Think of Babylon 5,000 years ago (Bottéro 1987). Listen to the prayer of a woman invoking the goddess of love: 'Take me! Don't be afraid! Get it up! Ishtar commands you!'

It would take me a long time to describe the infinite variety of these cults. I could, for instance, tell you about the extraordinary voluptuousness of Arabic eroticism (Chebel 1995), about pre-Islamic love poetry, and about the *Thousand and One Nights*, in which women were the rulers of desire (Chebel 1996). I could tell you about the early period of the rise of Islam, when physical love was seen as an expression of the will of God (Lamchichi 2006). Or I could tell you of the epic poems of the Arabian desert, such as the seventh-century tale of Layla and Majnun, which looks forward to the revolution in love that was to occur during the age of courtly love in the West.

Far from being the preserve of pagan cults, the praises of physical love are sung more than once by the great monotheisms, as in the *Song of Songs* and in the work of Muslim mystics. In his *Treatise of Love*, Ibn 'Arabi, for instance, writes that 'Contemplating the God who exists in women is the most perfect form of contemplation, and the most intense union is the act of love' (cited Lamchichi 2006: 61). It is, on the other hand, true to say that the idea that physical love (which is human, all too human) and the love of God can be one and the same has much more often been seen by the religions of salvation as a scandal, whilst the renunciation of the flesh has usually been seen as a precondition for the authentic love that leads us to God. And that is the starting point for the entire history of the feeling of love.

LOVE IN THE DARK

It all began almost 3,000 years ago – though I have to admit that the date is somewhat arbitrary – somewhere in what is now Iran when Zarathustra invented a completely new religion that evoked, for the first time in history, the possibility of salvation in the afterlife. To ensure one's salvation, one had to choose: Good or Evil, Light or Darkness. The idea of a divine light was present in most religions, and especially in those within the Indo-European tradition (Lambert 2007), but Zarathustra introduced a much more pronounced dualism. A few centuries later, but still in the same region, another prophet called Mani radicalized this dualism still further. Although these events occurred a very long time ago, their intellectual influence is still felt today. Take, for example, our intellectual habit of dividing everything into irreducible binary categories.

During the first centuries of the Christian era, the religious sect that followed the teachings of Mani was described as 'Manichean'. There were many other sects at this time, and they were all dualistic to a greater or lesser extent: there were Gnostics, the Encratites in Syria, the Marcionites, the Valentinians, the Mandeans, and so on, not to mention more individual forms of renunciation, such as the one preached by the Desert Fathers (Brown 1988). The underlying ideas were that the light of God was at war with the darkness of the world, that the world was by definition evil, and that anyone who wanted to be saved must renounce it. Sexuality was damned for two reasons. First, it aroused guilty desires, and, second, it perpetuated life on earth (Jonas 1963). This led to the emergence of the countless groups and communities that celebrated the mystical delights of human relationships that were devoid of any sensual pleasure, and of a love for God and one's neighbours in which there was no room for individual passion or individual desire.

These groups had a considerable influence on the way people thought, but that influence took many different forms. Sexuality obviously put up some resistance, but it was for a long time associated with night and with the freer, if not sulphurous, world of darkness (it is not just for practical reasons that modern couples make love at night). Their main influence was on Christianity. We tend to forget that early Christianity did not speak with one voice. For several centuries, its history was marked by clashes between extraordinarily different interpretations, many of them focused on love and sexuality, which were central to all these debates. The radical vision of the Manicheans proved very attractive to lots of Christians, including the young Augustine, who was so tormented by his dissolute sexual life. As he admits in his *Confessions* (1961 [387–8]: 43): 'I was inflamed with a desire for a surfeit of hell's pleasures. Foolhardy as I was, I ran wild with lust that was manifold and rank . . . I was foul to the core.' Tormented by the problem of evil, Augustine then read Plato – who showed him the path that led to Christianity – and became a virulent critic of the Manicheans.

The question of love had still not been settled. Christianity claimed to be a religion of love, or even *the* religion of love. It meant, of course, 'the love of God', which did not raise any problems. It also spoke of loving one's neighbour ('Love one another'), or of the universal charity the Scriptures called *agape*. But where did this legitimate love end, and where did the boundless ocean of passions and desires begin? The Manicheans had a very simple answer to that question, but many Christians found it impious because it was predicated upon the renunciation of the world. According to those who would soon denounce Manicheism as a heresy, Jesus was a god who became a man in order to save humanity despite sin and the realities of this world. The Gospels in fact contain two somewhat contradictory visions: one is obviously inspired by Manicheism, whilst the other takes a more open and understanding view of the materiality of worldly love. Because its outcome was uncertain, the debate therefore became even more intense. It soon became very heated, and it decided both the fate of love and its place in society. Although it now takes different forms, the same debate still goes on today and contrasts two types of love.

EROS IS NOT WHAT HE USED TO BE

I have briefly mentioned Plato, but only in passing. We now really do have to go back to Plato because he plays an immensely important role in the strange and tormented history of the feeling of love. His vision of love has, however, given rise to a number of misunderstandings. The first has to do with Eros. Plato made Eros a very important figure, but we now see his name on the windows of sex shops and the covers of porn magazines. What a come down! In Greek mythology, Eros is a god. Indeed, he is a major god. Phaedrus, who is one of the characters in *The Symposium*, which is Plato's famous treatise on love, says of the god Love (Eros) that he is 'oldest of the gods, so also he confers upon us the greatest benefits' (Plato 1951 [416 BC]: 42). This is a long way from pornography. Pausanias, another guest, tells Phaedrus that there are two forms of Love, and subsequent Platonist philosophy is based upon this distinction. According to Plato, the first form is 'common Love'. It is not in fact all that 'common' (and nor is it reducible to our modern eroticism). Whilst it does inspire the most carnal desires, it is above all a vital energy, and an essential starting point. Because, whether we like it or not, human beings are attracted to bodies (as Diderot later put it in distinctly male terms, 'there is something testicular about our most sublime feelings'[1]). Platonic love can, however, elevate our souls. They then encounter the heavenly Love or Eros who leads them into a higher world – the divine world of Beauty: 'Eros puts us on the road that leads to the astonishing revelation of Beauty itself' (Vernant 1996: 160).

Plato's sublimation of the flesh has been grossly over-simplified, especially when it is contrasted with Christian love. The Eros/*agape* dichotomy has become a cliché, but it is based on a misunderstanding, especially if we try to trace the origins of our eroticism back to Eros himself. There is another and more subtle misreading that relates Platonic love to an ascent (from common love to heavenly love) and contrasts it with Christian love, which descends from on high (the love of God that is spread by grace). Platonic love does take real human beings as its starting point and does allow them to reach a higher state. But in order to reach that higher state, they must already have been touched by the radiance of celestial beauty (see Simmel 1898), which is not too far removed from Christianity's grace. Plato's Eros is 'a luminous Aspiration' (Rougemont 1983 [1940]: 61). It is universal, and it does not cut us off from the world.

Because we overestimate the differences between Plato's Eros and Christianity's *agape*, we tend to forget that it was Plato who paved the way for Christianity. We also tend to overlook the fact that this dichotomy masks the further dichotomy between legitimate love and the passions, which has major social repercussions. Passion is the great alternative to love. We now see passion as just one more form of love, though it is admittedly more exciting than most, and contrast it with the peaceful delights of loving tenderness. Even so, we see it as one of the related emotions that we classify under the generic heading of 'love'. Now passion is by no means a feeling like any other. And the surprising story of passion will inspire the most turbulent episodes in the story I am telling.

In the most ancient times, little attention was paid to passion. It is not that there was no such thing as emotional effervescence. Far from it. It was, however, part of a mythical realm, and indeed

[1] Letter to Danilaille, 3 November 1760.

it played a part in founding that order and helping it evolve (Durkheim and Mauss 1963 [1903]). The ecstatic trances of witches, for example, provided answers to questions raised by the community (Makarius and Lévi-Makarius 1974). The defining feature of modern passion is, in contrast, its insistence on creating a world that is not of this world, a new world that is completely different from the world we know. This defining characteristic of passion was originally its marginality and negativity, rather as though it were an anarchic excess or a fever that was running out of control. The Ancient World and Plato himself did not have a good word to say about bad passions. But as society became more and more complex, it created more and more openings that allowed them a free rein. Physical desires and sentimental outbursts could not be completely controlled.

THE WAR BETWEEN VENUS OBSEQUENS AND VENUS ERYCINA

An anecdote about the war between two incarnations of Venus will illustrate the point I am trying to make. I obviously have to simplify it somewhat, as the Romans worshipped more than one Venus. Indeed, there were a lot of them. They were all love goddesses, but how could there be only one Venus when love took so many different forms, and when it was torn between tenderness and passion? Venus was the Roman equivalent to the Greek Aphrodite, and to the many other love goddesses found in other civilizations. The Babylonians had Ishtar, the Etruscans had Turna, the Hourrites had Shauska, the Incas had Tlahuizcalpantecuhtli, the Maya had Kukulcan, and the Icelanders had Sif, to name only a few. Idolatrous love has always been represented by a woman in all ages and all cultures.

For the moment, we will look at Ancient Rome. Rome had a problem with love from the very start. Roman society was characterized by its capacity for organization, the rigour of its laws, its military might and its patriarchal power. But these rather virile values were powerless against the powers of love. Especially as the history of Rome begins with a love story, as Pierre Grimal explains so well (Grimal 2002 [1988]). The gods themselves were defeated by the vestal virgins. Even Mars, the terrible god of war, fell in love with a woman descended from Aeneas. Aeneas himself was the son of the handsome shepherd Anchises and Aphrodite, who was swept off her feet as soon as she saw him. In a sense, it all begins with the violent passion that the goddess of love feels for a shepherd. Alarmed by the desires of the flesh and the impetuosity of the heart, power made every effort to control the cult of Venus, especially during the early period when Rome was both conservative and puritanical. These attempts ended in failure, especially in the countryside, where Venus presided over rituals associated with fertility. This was especially true in the region around Mount Eryx in Sicily, where a magnificent Venus of oriental origin worked miracles. Her cult attracted crowds, but it has to be said that there were other attractions on offer. Sacred prostitutes were, for example, made available to poor pilgrims. The Venus of Eryx was, as was only to be expected, extremely popular, and had the support of what we would now call public opinion.

In Rome, the promoters of religious orthodoxy took a dim view of this. They were secretly afraid of the unpredictable powers of this goddess, who was not like the others. It was said, for instance, that it was thanks to her protection that Carthage had been defeated. Rather than challenging the goddess or even ignoring her, Fabius Gurges therefore resolved to build a temple to her in 195 BC 'in the hope that this would appease her anger and ensure that she would encourage legitimate loves in future (Grimal 2002 [1988]: 64). He did, however, give her a name – Venus obsequens ('Graceful' or 'Indolent') – which was a clear indication that he did not want to have dealings with just any goddess, or just any representation of love. It is, however, a well-known fact that love cannot be governed by decree, and Venus Erycina, whose motives were supposedly lubricious, was still a cause for concern. The Senate therefore resolved to build a temple dedicated to Mens, god of reason, alongside her temple. 'An antidote to the orgiastic element in the cult of the Sicilian goddess, and to the madness she would unleash in men's hearts, was found in the purely intellectual religion of Mens' (Grimal 2002 [1988]: 66). It seems, however, that the power of Mens had little more effect than the decision to change the name of Venus Erycina. Despite all these precautions, the authorities had allowed 'the goddess of passionate love' to enter Rome (Grimal 2002 [1988]: 66). The Senate therefore drew up a plan to dedicate a statue to a very different Venus, namely the eminently chaste and respectable Venus Verticordia. The model for the statue was actually the winner of a 'real virtue contest' involving the hundred most chaste women in the aristocracy. One hundred years later, good society was, unfortunately, hit by scandals that demonstrated that desires could still enflame both bodies and hearts. The authorities therefore decided to enlarge the temple of the virtuous Venus Verticordia, and to move Venus Erycina to an outlying area far away from the Capitol. 'Worshippers now had to choose between the two goddesses. But it was the passionate and turbulent Venus who eventually won over their minds' (Grimal 2002 [1988]: 68).

GOOD AND BAD PASSIONS

Repressing the passions, and especially their most physical manifestations, is never easy. There is, however, another way of controlling them. Their vital energy can be diverted into other channels that keep the temptations of the flesh at bay. The Gnostics and the Manicheans provide the best examples. They were ruled by their hearts but that did not lead them into temptation because they had renounced the flesh in favour of the idea of a perfectly luminous world. They did not invent this model, and are merely its most radical interpreters. They did, on the other hand, have a more subtle influence, especially on the early Christians.

In the early centuries of Christianity, it was widely believed that the Apocalypse was imminent; the need for purification and redemption was therefore a matter of urgency. That there should have been outbursts of mystical passion is hence quite understandable. From the religious point of view, mystical passion is a good passion, if not an excellent passion. And yet all forms of passion introduce a discordant note into the Christian concept of love, which is dominated by *agape*, or a universal, charitable feeling that has its roots in the day-to-day life of the real world.

Leaving the passions of mysticism to one side, the issue of the renunciation of the flesh strikes a discordant note in itself. In the early Christian era, debates focused on the issue of sexuality: original sin became sexual, which was not originally the case

(Verdon 1996). Which is better from the religious point of view – celibacy and abstinence, which preserve purity in the expectation of salvation in the next life, or marriage, which symbolizes God's love for mankind? Theologians struggled with this question for hundreds of years, and reached a compromise solution: priests should remain celibate, but the laity could marry. To simplify the argument somewhat, the absence of the body cleared the way for mystical passions. The body could be kept under control and know no passion. The most surprising thing about this solution is not that love was divided into two, but that that it was divided in such a way as to give the clergy a monopoly on passion. Now, the very structure of passion means that it rebels against the world. And Christianity's programme accepts the world for what it is and loves it at all cost. According to Denis de Rougemont (whose famous *Love in the Western World* (1983 [1940]) introduces some powerful and innovatory ideas), the explanation is obvious: Christianity's passions actually derive from Indo-European paganism, which was greatly influenced by Manicheism.

The Manicheans were denounced as heretics and quickly disappeared from the scene, or so it seemed. But the underground influence of their thought continued to spread, and suddenly emerged in new forms, especially in Germany, Flanders and Champagne at the time of the millennium. This was especially true – and this becomes important in terms of the story I am telling – in Lombardy and southern France in the twelfth century thanks to the Cathar religion, which was based upon an ascetic ethics of chastity and a rejection of marriage.

I am not going to talk about the Cathars because it would take too long. Their religion, which claimed to be broadly inspired by Christianity, was subject to violent repression, and many of its followers ended up by being burned at the stake by the Inquisition. They regarded themselves as pure, and the world as evil, and their religion was therefore very austere. This explains why so many medievalists are critical of Denis de Rougemont's theses, even though they are detailed and convincing. They could not accept that such opposites – a gloomy Catharism and the bright colours of courtly love – could coexist. They did not understand that love is no stranger to such reversals, and that it always consists of opposites. Denis de Rougemont was right.

A New and Surprising Love

When we hear the words 'courtly love', we usually think of gallant knights and troubadours singing love poems. And all that is true. The Middle Ages were somewhat coarse (bawdy, if not obscene, when it came to love, and very crude indeed when it came to language), and such gentle manners come as something of a surprise. Courtly love began with poems, and literature invented a new form of love. Which is why scrupulous scholars began to ask more questions. Can we be sure that these fictional writings were in tune with actual realities? The simple answer is that we cannot. And is it self-evident that these gallant knights were always as virtuous as the code of love demanded? Did they just chastely hold their Ladies once they were in bed with them? We are not sure about that either. Courtly love combined a specific literary style and a code of behaviour (in the form of a mystical vision of love) with actual customs that were, to a greater or lesser extent, governed by that same code, especially in a medieval society that combined extreme religiosity with a never-ending quest for pleasure (Verdon 1996).

It is futile to try to pigeon-hole everything or to make too rigid a distinction between purely virtuous feelings on the one hand and libidinous hedonism on the other; if we do that, we will not understand anything, precisely because it is the dynamic and fluid relationship between the two that is important. Two very different but intersecting destinies will give us a better understanding of the logical connection between the two. The first is that of William, the powerful lord of Poitiers and a cousin to the kings of Europe. He liked to think of himself as a poet writing in the bawdy tradition that was so widespread at the time. The second – that of Robert d'Arbrissel – is its opposite in every respect. Although he was appointed an apostolic preacher by the Pope, Robert's inspiration was in fact drawn from Manicheism and in many respects prefigures the Cathar religion. In his virtuous sermons, he denounced the perversity and darkness of the world, and preached asceticism and detachment. He began his career as a hermit living in the forests, but he was soon surrounded by disciples. Communities began to emerge and crowds began to follow him.

They went barefoot, the men wore beards and they dressed in strange clothes – rather like the hippies of the 1960s, to judge by Denis de Rougemont's description (1983 [1940]: 355). Worshippers left their parish priests, and women left their husbands. For Robert was attractive to women, and took a special interest in their fate. In order to prove that he could resist temptation, he even ventured into the brothels and resolved to devote himself to converting prostitutes. He built colonies of huts around churches dedicated to the Virgin in remote areas far away from the towns. He either ran the colonies himself, or delegated the task to monks. After some unfortunate scandals, including a number of clandestine births, the Bishop of Rennes ordered Robert to set his house in order. His colonies eventually evolved into the Abbey of Fontrevault. It was unusual for the time in that its Superior was a woman. The fact that the monks submitted to the authority of an Abbess outlined a very different intellectual schema, which soon developed into the literature of courtly love: the knight submitted to his Lady (Rougemont 1983 [1940]).

To go back to William. He was extremely annoyed by Robert's success and even became jealous of him. The man was surrounded by such beautiful women and had proclaimed himself to be their guide! In William's view, it was obvious what was going on: all this was nothing more than an excuse for the most lascivious promiscuity. He therefore came up with the idea of making a mockery of Robert's colony and of constructing mock huts that would also allow him to satisfy his own sexual desires. He built a colony of little houses. They too were under the leadership of a woman, but the women who lived in them were really courtesans. The experiment did not, however, have the desired results. William's mind-set gradually changed, mainly because he compared his colony with the mystical ecstasies he had witnessed at Fontrevault. The change was, of course, most obvious in his poetry; whether or not he restricted his erotic activity to chaste kisses is still open to question. But the idea of a radiant but inaccessible Lady certainly provided the subject matter for an airy lyricism that could scarcely have found expression in the bawdy *fabliaux* he used to write. And so, William of Poitiers unexpectedly became a precursor of courtly love. Witness the poem entitled – and the title is a whole programme in itself – 'I will adore only her', in which he trembles with submissive emotion: 'I give myself to her, I surrender and she can add me to her list . . . I cannot live without her.' And William threatened to enter a monastery or to let himself die if his Lady, who was 'whiter than ivory', did not grant him the favour of just one kiss beneath a tree.

THE OUTBURST OF PASSION

The sudden emergence of courtly love, which was in many respects the antithesis of contemporary values, was an extraordinary event, and it is not easy to explain. As many specialists have shown, it was definitely a product of the convergence of very different influences. Arab-Muslim love poetry, and especially the variant that found its way into Europe via Andalusia, had introduced the refinements of a sublimated voluptuousness. It probably interacted with even older and more distant currents such as Indian Tantrism, with its promise of enlightenment through asceticism (Markale 1987). Jean Markale adds that the Celts must not be forgotten. They would play a major role in the subsequent history of love: the Breton romances picked up the theme of courtly love and give a new impetus to passion. But the influence of Celtic culture was probably also felt long before this, especially given the role played in it by women (the early mother-goddess, the sun goddess, glittering fairies).

The convergence of these (and many other currents) would not have triggered such an event had it not been for the almost revolutionary climate that prevailed in the twelfth century. After the nightmarish turbulence of the millennium, the relaxation of feudal and patriarchal bonds gave birth to 'a kind of advance Renaissance of individualism' (Rougemont 1983 [1940]: 112). Leaving aside the Cathars, criticisms of the established clergy, denunciations of marriage, outbursts of passion and various mystical experiments (both inside and outside the Church) were commonplace, given that this somewhat feverish atmosphere was dominated by the quest for an uncluttered spiritualism. The biography of Robert d'Arbrissel is a good example. It was, however, the underlying Manichean model, rather than any of these aspects, that played the decisive role and led to the emergence of something new. The promise of a world of light offered an escape from the intolerable burdens of this world. Love had always been torn in two directions, but the Catharism that invented courtly poetry changed everything by radically transforming the modalities of passionate love. It was no longer an anarchic eruption of voluptuousness that was fuelled by desire; it now gave birth to a philosophical and spiritual project. It gave birth to the idea of another world of light that was ideally perfect, and of a cosmogonic unity or self-unity that could finally be achieved.

Was the underlying model Manichean? Various currents derived from that intellectual tradition had in fact been secretly at work in society for hundreds of years, despite the seizure of power by the 'official' religions of Christianity and Islam. In the case of Islam, mention should be made of Suhrawardi of Aleppo, who also wrote in the twelfth century (Corbin 2001). Steeped in Greek – and especially Platonic – philosophy and greatly influenced by Zarathustra's dualism, he attempted to arrive at a synthesis of those currents and Islam. As he travelled from Iran to Syria, his mystical quest led him to elaborate a wisdom of enlightenment that would gradually reveal the Light of Lights. He talked a lot about love in, for instance, his *Vademecum of the Faithful in Love* (a more literal translation might be '*of the Love-Struck*' or '*of Lovers*'). The 'Faithful in Love' were in fact mystics, and their spirituality was basically a love-based mysticism (only pure, loving hearts can have access to the divine light). Slightly later, and on the other side of the Mediterranean, Dante said exactly the same when he described 'the faithful in love' in his *Vita nuova*. Neither the great poet's Lady nor Petrarch's is a purely earthly figure: there is something of the Madonna about both Beatrice and Laura.

To go back to Suhrawardi. He belongs to an intellectual tradition of mystics and poets who, like Al Hallaj and Ruzbehan de Shiraz in his 'Jasmin of the Faithful in Love', ask the same questions. Their rhetoric of love and chivalry does recall the work of the courtly poets, but the purely spiritual question is their dominant theme. 'The faithful in love' are primarily mystics who invented a new religion. And it was that that led to their downfall. The Ulemas who were the guardians of orthodox Islam denounced their ideas, and Saladin had Suhrawardi put to death.

That was the tragic thing about these various Manichean tendencies: their radical visions were very attractive, but they offered no solutions here on earth, and they did not succeed in putting down deep roots. Throughout history, they were regularly denounced as heresies, and then violently repressed and stamped out. That was the fate of the Cathars, who were the victims of the first crusade to be waged inside Christendom. But a single event transformed the future of love, and spiritual mysticism was metamorphosed into a mystique of love. In a sense, the defeated Cathar religions re-emerged in a new form, and now provided the ideological backdrop for a new religion of love.

This explains all the courtly code's puzzling features: the extreme, symbol-laden ritualization, the strangely gentle manners, the sentimental spirituality, the art of self-restraint, the rejection of easy solutions and profane pleasures, the elevation of the soul, and above all the adoration of women, who were put in a position of superiority in a savagely macho period. Then there is the critique of marriage: passion is something that develops outside marriage and in opposition to marriage (it should be recalled that, for the Cathars, marriage was a major indication of a compromise with the world of darkness). Courts of Love presided over by great ladies such as Eleanor of Aquitaine debated this serious question at great length: can, in exceptional circumstances, a husband feel real passion for his wife? The debates were lively, but the answer was usually in the negative. Real passions would inevitably be destroyed inside the worldly institution of marriage.

THE PLEASURES OF RESTRAINT

The knight who was in love with his Lady had to go through the interminable ordeals she set him, not without some sadism . . . That did not matter: a pure heart that had been exposed to the light of love could bear all wounds and overcome the most unexpected obstacles. The knights of love were able to perform amazing feats, but the hardest ordeal of all came as they finally got close to their Ladies. The courtly code defined those stages of the journey in great detail. The knight's first reward came when his Lady looked at him (her gaze was the 'gateway to the luminous soul'). She then touched his hand before they finally kissed in the orchard. It was only now that the knight of love could begin to dream of entering his Lady's chamber. We have to be careful here. We are not in today's society, where 'Do you want to come back for a coffee?' is all it takes to let the suitor know that everything is going to be easy from now on. There were more ordeals to come. They were far from minor ordeals and formed part of a slow, codified sequence. The suitor had to go through the ordeal of *assag* (submission to his Lady) to prove that the light of love shone within him, and that he was capable of displaying a chaste restraint now that, after so much waiting and so many ordeals, the attractions of the Lady's physical beauty seemed at last to be within reach (Nelli 2005 [1963]). He had to sleep for a whole night in his Lady's bed, touching her only with his eyes. He might receive a kiss beneath the tree in the orchard, but it was almost chaste. He might have to stare at her naked body, or the couple might have to sleep side by side – naked but without touching. The actual forms taken by courtly love often ignored this austere sub-text. Many troubadours were not satisfied with such ethereal encounters, and often described less angelic physical meetings and more feverish embraces (but always took care to avoid penetration). But the most audacious initiatives were always taken at the suggestion of the Lady.

Troubadours and courtly lovers often distanced themselves from this underlying mysticism. But the surprising or paradoxical thing is that, the closer they came to their impossible goal, the more they discovered the new and strange pleasures, or even a secret *jouissance*, of restraint, of the art of preliminaries and of the sophisticated delights of seduction. Moving away from the desired object heightened desire, and ritualizing the stages of the final approach to the Lady opened up a world of unexpected sensations. And so, the unthinkable happened: courtly love turned into its opposite. The Cathars' gloomy ideas about the body and its pleasures were forgotten as poets began to concentrate on the divine light. It was possible to find a more sensual light here on earth, in the present tense of the gentle well-being of caresses that promised greater joys to come. Courtly love had become a joyous and lively theory, and the art of gallant good manners began to be celebrated by poets. That is how we remember it; hence the name, which is acquired at a later stage. It was originally known in *langue d'Oc* as *fin' amour*, meaning 'perfect love'. And that implies a very different programme.

This episode demonstrates the extent to which the contradictory aspects of love are interrelated, and their surprising ability to change places. Nothing could be more dialectical than this fluid emotion. Courtly love has bequeathed us an enormous legacy, often in indirect and hidden ways. Its most obvious legacy can be seen in the refined manners of the seductions and gallantry that gave birth to a real pre-Renaissance and that inspired, in later centuries, 'the most splendid of Western literary works' (Rougemont 1983 [1940]: 92). Literature is not simply an artistic reflection of a given period: it prefigures the world to come, and it is a very concrete tool that can be used to transform the existing world. It is therefore not surprising to find that it was not until long after the event that it became possible to appreciate the real effects of courtly love. It took centuries for courtly values, which derived from a heresy that rejected marriage, to become enshrined within Christian marriage.

We are also heir to many other heritages, some of them political. It was in the twelfth century that people began to believe that the individual could assert his individuality, and above all invent his own world and create his own values, though it was not until much later that this became obvious (Le Bart 2008). The courtly experiment provides one of the first models for this individuality: the hero can escape the reality of this world and can achieve the goals he has set himself. This is in fact a very strange model for individuality, as it is intimately bound up with someone else. And it is not the individual model that is remembered by history; the model that history remembers created many more problems for the social bond and, of course, for love.

The last bequest from courtly love and the Breton romances that continued its tradition that I would like to emphasize is more specifically religious.

THE TWO FACES OF THE BELOVED

Celtic religion loved women, no matter whether they were fairies or goddesses (Markale 1987). It was not the only religion to do so. The figure of the mother-goddess is a constant in very many belief-systems. Her maternal warmth or even gentleness makes her stand out from the male gods, who are usually more warlike or aggressive. 'Male' and 'female' are mental categories that have existed since the beginning of time (Lambert 2007). Christianity had a problem with this cultural division of the world. Jesus himself did not have any problems with it, as he tended to be sympathetic to women (Héritier 1996), but the first Christian communities were established in Roman society and within a Judaic tradition, both of which were very patriarchal. The new religion could not escape that context completely. Male figures therefore took pride of place in the divine pantheon, and the pantheon of the apostles was almost exclusively male. Mary was one the very few exceptions, but her presence in the Gospels always remains very furtive. She was not the object of any particular cult during the early centuries of Christianity. When a cult did begin to develop, the Church Fathers condemned it. In the fourth century, Ambrose and Epiphanius made specific appeals for an end to the worship of the Virgin. They failed to realize that this is not how religious issues are decided. There was an underlying popular need for a religion that was less harsh, and it inspired the search for a female figure. And was not Christianity supposed to be a loving religion? A woman would be in a better position to bring out the gentle side of that love, and related beliefs abounded in female figures of the deity. The pagans had their goddesses (Venus was still very present in people's minds) and the Celts had many more. So too did the Gnostics who referred to ancient mother-goddesses and worshiped Sophia (Markale 1987).

The Church therefore had to bow to popular pressure, and the Council of Ephesus declared the cult of Mary legitimate. Ephesus, of all places! This was either ironic, or a calculated gesture. The city was

> The unchallenged capital of the cult of the mother-goddess, previously honoured as Artemis and now worshipped in the form of the famous Scythian Diana, who was at once cruel and kind, a virgin and a sensualist, divine and human, and both inaccessible and close at hand. She was a thinly disguised version of the sun goddess of the early Indo-Europeans crossed with the more lascivious Mesopotamian goddess of sexuality, beauty and love. (Markale 1987: 197)

Mary was of course given a much more diaphanous appearance and was not surrounded by the same ambiguity. And the cult of Mary was on a modest scale until the twelfth century, when there was a real explosion of various forms of Mariolatry, rather as though this desire had been repressed for too long.

Even the game of chess saw the appearance of a new piece when the Queen became the major element and relegated the poor King, who could only move one square at a time, to an honorific role. The French equivalent is *la dame*, which derives from the Latin *domina*, and that was the word that slaves used to describe their mistresses (Grimal 2002 [1988]). The queen or *dame* was a somewhat inaccessible higher being who was both attractive and luminous, and she became much more important when she took on the features of courtly love's Lady. The inevitable crystallization (I use Stendhal's term very loosely) came about when these many currents converged in a fervour that was ambiguous but that remained, for official purposes, profane. Many Christians were, like St Francis of Assisi, drawn to the mysticism of chivalrous love. The Church owed it to itself to intervene so as not to be outflanked. And the only way it could counter-attack was by promoting the cult of the Virgin. It soon became extremely widespread:

> She was found in every church and invaded every altar. She was the perfect, exemplary saint. Her litanies were sung everywhere. She was prayed to almost more often than her son. She was given sumptuous dwelling places. She was depicted as a queen. She was crowned. She was draped in mantles decorated with god and embroidery. The processions held in her name began to follow truly labyrinthine routes. She often appeared to her worshippers. She told them her secrets. She cured incurable diseases. (Markale 1987: 212)

She was Mary, the Holy Virgin, but she was also the Good Lady, the Lady in White (a common image in mythology and folklore) who brought a little charitable kindness. And on the pediments of chapels, churches and cathedrals, she often became 'Our Lady'. The singular '*ma*' *dame* ('My Lady') of courtly love was turned into a plural (*notre dame*) that was more in keeping with a universal *agape*. But make no mistake about it: all these strictly orthodox Our Ladies are thinly disguised versions of the astonishing courtly Lady.

THE SECOND WAVE OF PASSION

Dear Isolde, I don't know if you realized the full importance of the 'Tristan' romance for the history of love when you chose your pseudonym. At first sight, the story simply seems to extend the themes of courtly poetry to the forests of Brittany. But remember what happened first: a mystical cult was transmuted into nothing more than a new and pleasing vision of love, and that vision came to be associated with a derivative form of belief in a less ambiguous Lady who could be suspected neither of voluptuousness nor of heresy. That transformation came at a high price: passion was no longer a force that sought to change society.

Thanks to a new paradox (and love is no stranger to paradox), it took a detour via the sacred to breathe new life into a profane passion. The mystery-based spirituality of the Celtic tradition offered the ideal solution. The schema was rather different from that of courtly love. Whilst the beloved was more luminous than ever, the world was harsh, dark and full of ordeals that no one had chosen. Winning the fair lady is no longer the point. On the contrary, it all begins with the sin of adultery: desire was too strong. The lovers refuse to give up their love and, despite all the attractions of their material situation, they flee society for the sake of love, and die as a result. The moral of the story is that complete love can win only if the lovers die. That is not, you might say, a very enticing prospect. But you have to understand that it is a model, and that the model has immense power. The Manichean back-drop is there (love is the divine light, the world is evil and has to be renounced in the name of love), but that is not the important point. Something different is beginning to emerge: passion can invent a new world for lovers. This is a counter-world, and entering it means leaving this world behind. A more attractive and luminous world can be created if an emotional impulse can free us from the intolerable burdens of the world in which we currently live. And we also often dream a secret dream that could not be shared by Tristan and Isolde, whose passion brought them no happiness in this world. A new and luminous world exists somewhere in the beyond, and we can make it real. We can be as one if we share the same emotions in the intimacy of the here and now.

Love therefore becomes a very meaningful madness that is quite 'unlike the Christian conception, which claims that man was made in God's image, and possesses, like God, the essential faculty of rationality' (Demartini 2005: 147). The faculty of reason has to be abandoned by anyone who wants to escape from the world and to bring about a subversive break; passion had obvious revolutionary implications (Alberoni 1994). It does not, however, require the violent weapons that are used in most revolutions. Courtly poetry and the Breton romances tell us that an exchange of glances is all it takes to allow two souls to fuse immediately and to leave behind the world around them.

ROMANCE

The new model's power is also bound up with a new literary form. Courtly love was popularized by poetry, which evoked its delicate manners by singing its praises. The romance introduced a very different dynamic. It begins with a sin, and the multiple uncertainties this opens up lend themselves to lots of different plots. The problematic is in fact always the same and it contrasts two orders of reality: the potential reality of a dream world created by passion, and the contingencies of existing society. In most versions of the *Tristan* romance, there is almost no tension because we know that pure love must be victorious. The romance form becomes increasingly dominant as it opens up more and more uncertainties and possibilities. That is what gives modern love stories their density and richness. Even for today's movies and television serials, the romance form is still an important tool when it comes to building future forms of love (Chalvon-Demersay 1996). The romance or novel is one of the laboratories in which the future is designed (Barrère and Martuccelli 2009).

This extraordinary adventure began with *Tristan*, but so did other adventures. The novelty of *Tristan* is the way it turns the madness of love into a madness of words by outlining 'the contours of a space for the "I" and creating a semblance of intimacy' (Demartini 2005: 149). The Breton romances explore subjectivity and in a sense invent modern individuality. They do so by using pronouns, amongst other devices, to establish new supports for our personal identities, but above all by staging the internal dialogue that results from a conflict between the two orders of reality. The subject was constructed at the centre of the divide between the two, where it could act as its own mirror. The 'emergence of a feeling, of a song and, at the same time, a subject' made it a real 'machine for imagining characters' (Demartini 2005: 145–6). At a deeper level, the romance form encourages introspection, and it is that that guaranteed its success in later centuries, when it scrutinized in ever-greater detail the minutiae of real life and the innermost recesses of the individual's secret thoughts.

Until then, love's only battle had been with love itself. It was a battle to decide what best suited humanity: common love or heavenly love, universal *agape* or mad passion, mystical passion or a physically human passion? But with the approach of the Renaissance, a new character took the stage and soon had the starring role in our play: the rational individual. But before we tell the story of love's next defeat, we need to make one thing clear. At the beginning of our story, we travelled a little as we followed in the footsteps of Mani in Iran and of Suhrawardi of Aleppo. The rest of my story will, however, be confined to the West, and I must apologize for this. Many of my examples will be taken from France, which is the country I know best. They are, on the other hand, representative of the similar events that took place at the same time all over Europe. I would have liked to paint a broader picture that also took in Africa or Asia to demonstrate the extent to which love has always preoccupied the hearts and minds of the people of all civilizations, to look at the unusual plots that have been woven all over the world, and at the emotional and sentimental wonders that have been invented. That would take more than one book. If we wish to understand the keys to the mystery, we have to take a detailed look at the mechanisms that produce different forms of love. We have to choose between a systematic description of various cultures, and an understanding of the dynamic that lies at the heart of love. I have made my choice.

I will therefore be talking about only one cultural space. The West has no superiority in itself, and it has no lessons to teach anyone. Indeed, and as Montaigne already knew, it may have a great deal to learn from other cultures as it coldly surveys them from a distance. History is, however, what it is and it cannot be rewritten. There is nothing specifically Western or specifically Christian about the mystical attempt to sublimate the flesh (it actually began in pagan Antiquity (Guillebaud 1998)). We can see the same tendency in Indian Tantrism, in the China of Confucius, and in the Sufism we have inherited from the Bedouin (Chebel 1995). What was a global trend did, however, take different forms in different civilizations and evolved at different speeds at different times. And, as chance would have it, it was in the West that circumstances inverted the radically emotional impulse that inspired the Catharist heresy. This gave birth to courtly love and created the model for a great profane passion. It created the model for neither the art of voluptuousness nor love poetry, both of which were already highly developed elsewhere, often in more sensual forms. But it did provide the model for a profane passion that suggested the idea of creating a counter-world. Thanks to a second coincidence, this intellectual revolution took place just as a debate about how a society should be governed was getting under way and just as the idea of an autonomous individual was beginning to emerge, as we can see from the *Tristan* romance. And, thanks to a third coincidence, the West was on the point of entering the long historical period during which it would rule the world and during which its intellectual categories became dominant in every domain (Goody 2006). It now seems, of course, that this period is coming to an end and that Asia, in particular, is developing more rapidly – and not only in the economic domain. This long period of Western dominance has, however, bequeathed the world a cultural heritage that has acquired a universal value. The immense intellectual and political task of taking an inventory and sorting out what is specific to the West, and what is truly universal, is now being undertaken, but that is not what this book is about. Where love is concerned, intellectual and political debates can never decide anything: hearts will do that. And for the moment, the conclusion is obvious: the forms of love that result from the story I am going to tell really have taken on a universal value, and are rarely challenged.[2] At times, certain institutions (and especially the family) do serve as the guardians of traditions that are deeply rooted in specific cultures. But when they do so, passionate love, which is a product of the story I am telling, intervenes like some subversive ferment. In modern India, the on-going revolution in love uses its vocabulary, and women are using 'Bollywood romances' in a bid for liberation. And those romances did not come from nowhere. But let us not get ahead of ourselves.

[2] According to Olivier Abel (2006) the West's model for love is central to its influence.

2

At the Crossroads

The twelfth century was an age of revolution, and its revolutions were triggered by two new forms: passionate love and individual subjectivity (Morris 1972). The major upheavals that ensued could obviously have taken a very different course. The duel between love and individuality had begun, but its outcome was not a foregone conclusion.

Misunderstandings about Individuality

How did reason succeed in marginalizing love? It could not have done so were it not for a historical break or a radical change in the way society worked, and this is the source of some widespread misunderstandings. Modern society is often described as 'individualistic' because the individual is king. Individuals enjoy freedom of choice and are in control of their future, which is no longer a destiny (Singly 2005). This new type of society is contrasted with the traditional societies that the great anthropologist Louis Dumont (1983) describes as 'holistic' (from a Greek root that refers to the idea of a totality). Holistic societies are societies in which the individual merges into a social totality. The idea that holistic and individualistic societies work in completely different ways has, however, recently been called into question. Some say that the individual is not as free as we might think in these individualistic societies, and was probably freer than we think in holistic societies. We have here a misunderstanding that has to be cleared up. The official rules of the game are being confused with the concrete reality experienced by the individual, and this is what the historical break was all about (Le Bart 2008). Individuals are indeed much less free than they might imagine in this individualistic society. I have pointed out in a different study (Kaufmann 1995) that, the more open the space (such as the beach), the more peoples' main activity consists in producing collective behavioural norms. Conversely, individuals had a lot of room for manoeuvre in holistic societies; the fact that there were collective laws did not prevent them from reaching ad hoc arrangements to suit their own needs. The historical break we are talking about concerned the rules of the social game, and not concrete individuals. To simplify the argument, let us say that the difference between these types of society revolves around this question: where are the meanings of right and wrong, and true and false, defined? In a holistic society, individuals live within collective structures – most of them religious – that give them all the same answers to these questions. The individual's personal consciousness is 'hung up outside' (Vernant 1996: 226). In today's society, in contrast, it is up to the individual to choose, and to go on choosing, in every domain, between thousands of products, thousands of ideas, thousands of ways of going about things, thousands of moral principles, and thousands of people. The social bond has become elective, even when it comes to love, and this greatly complicates things (think of internet dating: how can you choose the right man or woman from the countless 'profiles' that are on offer?). In holistic societies, taking these decisions was not a matter for individuals. Their choices were pre-determined, either by their position within a kinship system or by the families who weighed up potential dowries and arranged marriages between inheritances rather than individuals. And that is why passionate love had a revolutionary impact at the level of individual emancipation, and why plays and novels talked about it for hundreds of years.

The twelfth century was an important moment in the slow emergence of this new form, and the autonomous individual gradually became the pivot around which the workings of society revolved. The individual who was soon to become so central to the functioning of society had yet to emerge, and there were several different potential models on offer. The fate of the world depended upon which model was chosen. The *Tristan* romance offered a particularly attractive model: an individual who was in love, capable of taking the initiative, and able to perform incredible individual feats but who was also, despite himself, in the process of forging a powerful emotional bond. That model was not adopted, or at least not in any real sense. It had several flaws: it implied a revolutionary change (creating an individual counter-world is not exactly the best way to organize collective life) and it offered no real future (the couple were madly in love, but social death was their only future). The figure of the impassioned individual looked both provocative and marginal from the very outset. Its origins were in fact heretical, and that is no coincidence. For Christianity, which had been the dominant religion since the third century, passion was acceptable only if it took the form of the most spiritual mysticism. Of course it defined itself as the religion of love, but was based upon a universal *agape*. Although its *agape* structured the social bond by negating the self, it did so in a different way, and displayed none of the exclusivity that divorces love from society. God commanded all men to love their neighbours. Christianity therefore rejected any model of the individual that was based upon amorous passion, and helped to construct a very different model.

THE IRRESISTIBLE RISE OF REASON

The idea of reason goes back a long way. Like the idea of love, it has always referred to contradictory contents, and this means that it has had an eventful history. For the Greek philosophers, reason was the *logos*, meaning both 'discourse' (the Greeks loved to talk) and 'theory' (they also loved intellectual speculation). The Romans, for their part, were primarily organizers who cared about clearly defined laws and strict accountability. *Logos* now became *ratio*, which referred to the idea of calculation as well as that of rationality. The Christians refused to be left behind, and went so far as to 'sanctify reason' (Nemo 2004: 60). 'In the beginning was the Word', says the Gospel According to St John. God is Light and Truth, and He deposits both within each of us with the help of the Holy Spirit, who underwent many mutations. The Holy Spirit is one of the three forms in which God manifests Himself (the others are the Father and the Son), and often acts as the mediator between God and men. That is why it is often depicted in the shape of a dove: it descends from heaven. The Spirit mediates in many different ways (allowing, for instance, Mary to give birth without having had sexual relations), but its most important function is to act as the bringer of faith and knowledge, and the two are very closely related because knowledge is divine. Things began to fall apart when some intellectuals, who were steeped in Greek philosophy, began to describe the capacity for rationality (which was, they believed, a gift from God) as something autonomous. They believed that they were still Christians in the full sense of the word, and were convinced that the new truth they were trying to uncover was God's truth. But they were in fact beginning to establish new mental categories and to develop a subversive mode of thought. Abelard, who famously fell in love with Héloïse, was already convinced that theology could be developed into a real science, and had developed many intellectual tools to make it one. A major divide was opening up within medieval scholasticism between the purely spiritual tradition and a new form of philosophy that was becoming more and more autonomous (Iogna-Prat 2005).

Christianity is a religion of love, and it is based upon the *agape* that cements the social community together (Boltanski 1990). It invokes a universal magnanimity which, as Georg Simmel quips somewhere, commands us to love 'God and earthworms', or, in other words, the whole of God's creation. On the other hand, Christianity took a very dim, if not hostile, view of the passions. They offended both the world order and reason. St Augustine gives the example of desire, which suddenly flares up and causes the male organ to become erect. In his view, such desire is to be condemned as it is a sign of a lack of will power. An individual who wished to be in control of his life had to rely upon (divine) Reason. But in about the thirteenth century, the ancient idea of Reason came to be more and more closely associated with individual consciousness and the individual conscience. All over the Europe of scholasticism, scholars began to define the consciousness as 'an autonomous agency of knowledge and not just judgement' (Boureau 2005: 291).

Although they did not know it, these scholars were beginning to elaborate the idea of individual autonomy. Living in an imperfect world, they told themselves that any individual who had been enlightened by these new ideas had been touched by grace and was a forerunner of a new humanity that could live in accordance with the will of God. The Church was now faced with the 'constant demands of individual discoveries of the truth' (Boureau 2005: 302). Its response was blanket censorship. It was too late: the dynamic of a rationally based individual autonomy was outside its control.

THE COLD ENLIGHTENMENT

The Church had to keep an eye on two worrying developments: the new emphasis on individual autonomy was a threat to the institutional order, and the irresistible rise of Reason was taking on philosophical overtones. The final outcome was the intellectual apotheosis of the Age of Enlightenment. The Enlightenment tended to secularize everything, including sentiment, which it tried to reduce to sensibility. The eighteenth century rejected all mythologies and was interested only in understanding nature. It either denounced the passions as instincts that had run wild or reduced them to a subtle game (sophisticated banter in the style of Marivaux and similar dangerous liaisons). Sentimentality's social role had been called into question, and it would never be the same again. Love was on the point of losing the greatest battle in its long history. In the new, rationally based intellectual order, love was marginalized and relegated to a separate sphere. Love offered consolation and mended broken hearts, and became the basis of a private world of intimate relationships. Just as the individual began to take the starring role, the individual was divided into two.

The Enlightenment programme was a programme for an extraordinary intellectual revolution, and it opened up exciting prospects. It is still of burning contemporary relevance to the fight against all kinds of obscurantism. Its democratic, tolerant and universal values are vital weapons in the fight against contemporary injustices and the breakdown of society into groups that hate each other without knowing anything about each other. We need the wisdom of the Enlightenment more than ever before. The only problem is that there was no room for love in the individual model that was developed to make this revolution possible. Everything that could be related to love – the development of a greater sensitivity towards others, an ethics of generosity – was put on one side, as was love's political potential. Love was certainly a central topic of discussion, but only insofar as it was a personal matter. In the feverish climate of the times, few objected to the way love was relegated to a secondary role because Reason opened up such exciting prospects. The Enlightenment understood Reason to mean knowledge in the noblest of senses. Reason implied both a passion for discovery and the belief that the constant progress of knowledge would create a new world (and even, it was thought, a better world).

Sadly, it proved difficult to apply Reason in all its pomp. It was soon discovered that Reason was based upon a critical way of thinking that systematically deconstructed all established truths. That, of course, was precisely what politics did not want: politicians need clear points of reference if they are to be able to take action. And the scholars rapidly came into conflict with the politicians of the day (Badinter 1999, 2002, 2007). The politicians assimilated Reason, but their definition of Reason was much narrower, much more pragmatic and had little to do with the adventure of knowledge. The great virtue of the idea of rights and law was that it paved the way for democracy; its great vice was that it encouraged the selfish calculations of economics. Love was excluded in the name of an ideal that would never be able to achieve its greatest ambitions.

In Search of Good Passions

And yet this development took place at a time when a great deal of thought was being devoted to the political role of the passions. In the sixteenth and seventeenth centuries in particular, philosophers reflected upon the passions, tried to understand and to classify them, to decide which were good and which were bad, and to determine which of the 'good' passions could be used to forge a harmonious social bond. Many treatises on the passions were published, and they became best-sellers. Writing from a Christian perspective, Edward Reynolds, for instance, divorced the destructive passions from those that could be a source of peace of mind and satisfaction in his *Treatise of the Passions and Faculties of the*

Soule of Man (1640). Thomas Wright analyses how moderated passions could become 'instruments of virtue' in his *The Passions of the Minde in Generall* (1601). 'Moderated passions' appeared to be the appropriate emotions for anyone who wished to govern the world.

These theories were developed at a time when the break-up of religious holism was opening up new spaces for politics. The quest for 'good passions' in fact masked some serious fears that princes might be overcome by bad passions that would turn them into despots. At this time, men were easily overcome by passion. Indeed, the passions were cultivated as so many virtues that signalled the differences between the aristocracy and the masses. Nothing, it seemed, could be more important than chivalric honour and glory.

Both those passions were precisely what the wise administration of men demanded by the new state did not want. They were therefore described as dangerous passions, and condemned as such. The state had to find a calmer passion that could supply energy without encouraging misdemeanours. It was found in the lower depths of the mentality of the times, in what had previously been regarded as the most shameful passion of all, namely avarice, greed and love of money. Within the space of a few decades, what had been noble became hateful, and what had been base came to be seen as the source of everything that was praiseworthy. The most shameful vice was transformed into the supreme virtue. Once again, the magical transformation of an idea into its opposite was about to change the face of the world. And the shameful passion that become the sovereign virtue was the quest for profit or self-interested calculation.

AN IDEA THAT WOULD CHANGE THE FACE OF THE WORLD

The term 'interest' did not originally have the meaning we now give it. In the sixteenth century, the notion of interest was not closely bound up with the world of money, and 'referred, on the contrary, to all human aspirations, although it did imply that there was an element of reflection and self-interested calculation in the choice of the means used to achieve them' (Hirschman 1980: 34). 'Self-interest' was a sort of practical equivalent to Reason, which was an elusive concept that could not easily be expressed in more concrete terms. For Machiavelli, self-interest and reason of state were synonymous. In 1638, the duc de Rohan opened his essay *De l'Intérêt des princes et Etats de Chrétienté* ('On the Interest of the Princes and States of Christendom') with the precept: 'Princes command peoples, and self-interest commands princes.' He meant that practical reason had to ward off the dangerous excesses of the passions. He later added that:

> in matters of state, one's behaviour must not be governed by those disordered desires that often encourage us to do things that are beyond our strength, nor by the violent passions that upset us in different ways, depending on how they possess us ... but by our self-interest. Self-interest, guided by reason alone, must be the rule that governs our actions.

The term had, however, long had another and very different meaning too. It referred to the income that was derived from lending money. Perhaps the idea of calculation was implicit in both these usages. Whatever the truth of the matter, the semantic shift occurred in a short space of time. 'Interest' suddenly took on a more economic meaning, and came to refer to rational calculations that had pragmatic and profitable goals. The new coinage immediately provoked 'real intellectual excitement' and 'it was assumed that this wonderful notion could resolve all problems' (Hirschman 1980: 48). This conjuring trick was possible only because the term retained its old intellectual prestige at the very time that it acquired a very different content. And it took some skilful conjurors to bring off the trick. But there were also a lot of people who did not realize what was going on. Once it had been renamed 'interest', the shameful passion of greed could be transformed into a cardinal virtue. The old passion was hateful because it was the antithesis of the idea of grandeur and nobility; greed was mean and petty-minded. Once it had been rebaptised, it became a calm, peaceful emotion that was far removed from the exalted passions that posed such a threat to the governance of the state. Hence the appeals to calculation and moderation, which are the essential characteristics of any administration.

The idea that affairs of state and social life should be based upon the vision of an individual who was motivated by self-interest became embodied in a personality-type that was 'less luxuriant, less unpredictable and, ultimately, more "one-dimensional"' (Hirschman 1980: 119). Interest could be both measured and mastered. Men who were guided by self-interest would, it was believed, allow the state to develop an operational rationality.

None of this was inevitable. Love could, perhaps, have become our guide to worldly affairs. Reason and the great adventure of knowledge could, perhaps, have retained their central position. But when it came to the direct management of human affairs, Reason was too abstract a tool, and it eventually become subordinate to the political. And the political then reduced it to meaning 'interested calculation' in the narrowest of senses, so much so that politics itself was dispossessed by economics. The economy in fact developed into a self-regulating system, and was theorized by Adam Smith, who soon came to be in a very central position. The governance of the world was no longer a topic for discussion: the market economy was modelled on the rational individual, and the world therefore functioned automatically.[1] We obviously still discuss value, the meaning of good and evil, and the importance of the passions, just as they did in Plato's day. But we do so mainly because we enjoy playing with words and ideas, and because such discussions are a source of intellectual–aesthetic pleasure that has little to do with the way the world actually works. The economy is self-regulating and the world therefore works automatically. The market economy was not, of course, a purely political invention. It was already in existence, and it was both active and calculating, especially in certain cities in medieval Italy, Spain and Flanders. The pilgrims who flocked to Jerusalem made twelfth-century Venice rich. But by the seventeenth century, Venice controlled only 'very limited sectors of trade, finance and international commerce, and these were mere surface layers' (Castel 2002 [1995]: 202). The market economy was chosen as an instrument of government long before it came to dominate society, and it was because it had been chosen as an instrument of government that

---

[1] Rationality was gradually reduced to meaning calculated interest in the narrowest of senses. Adam Smith's subject still developed, for example, an operational rationality; the subject described by Ricardo and Malthus was nothing more than a calculating individual obsessed with his own interests.

it came to dominate society. Eighteenth-century debates about the passions and self-interest were not idle chatter by any means. Capitalism did not have to be asked twice to take the place it had been offered. Capitalism was eager to express its dynamism, and was just waiting to be asked. But it could not have played this role if politics itself had not made it central to politics, if the political had not succeeded in recuperating the fine model of the coldly rational individual that the philosophers had developed, if the political had not succeeded in reducing that model to the dimensions of a narrowly calculating individual, and if love had not been marginalized.

Two Models

The later episode that takes us up to today's financial crisis is worth a brief description. The economists who had become the new masters of the universe dreamed up increasingly sophisticated mathematical models in which there was no room for what little passion remained. They refined their vision of human beings until it was as dry as a mathematical equation. You have to imagine the full implications of this. As I pointed out in the article you mention in your letter, society has given economics a central social role, but economics itself is based upon an incredibly reductive vision of what human beings are. And it is a hateful vision, because a calculating individual is inevitably going to be selfish. It is also a false vision because human beings are sentimental creatures who are eager to give their lives a wider meaning. Putting all the emphasis on this miserable facet of the human personality is simply unacceptable, and it is therefore not surprising that we hear so many complaints about promises that have not been kept. There has probably never been as much mental and emotional unhappiness as there is in our opulent society. This appears to be a paradox, but it is not, and all we have to do to understand it is go back to the expulsion of love.

'Economic theory's individual' is no more than 'one of a whole series of other possible models' (Caillé 2009: 178). There are many other visions of what human beings are, and many of them have to do with a commitment to love. It is true that love has never succeeded in coming up with a viable alternative. This is because it is torn between conflicting tendencies, and has not been able to make them reach a minimal compromise (as happened when Reason was reduced to meaning self-interest). And yet even its conflicting forms do converge. *Agape* is calm whereas passion can be insane, but they both take us out of ourselves. They make us forget the selfish little self that has become so introverted. *Agape* does so by appealing to an altruistic generosity and to universality, whilst passion does so by heightening our emotions and individualizing the man or woman we love. Leaving aside these differences, the affect that helps us to forget about ourselves also creates a social bond, and that is the important point. Whatever form it takes, and whatever its object may be, love defines individuals by binding them to other individuals. Love produces bonds, and not just bonds between people. Charles Taylor (1989) analyses how, in the romantic ideal, this perspective makes us part of a harmonious world, whereas the rational individual remains a detached observer who seems to watch everything from the outside. Passion introduces us to a new world that is full and complete, as opposed to a reality that is fractured and divisive. *Agape*, for its part, tries to glue the scattered fragments of that reality back together again through self-sacrifice. I do not, however, wish to over-idealize the 'loving individual' model. That model can leave less room for individual freedom, precisely because it forges bonds. 'The loving self expands through giving itself away to the loved object' (Bauman 2003: 9), whereas liquid society's 'man with no bonds' (Bauman 2003: vii; cf. Bauman 2006) is completely autonomous. The rational individual is not just cold and calculating; his detachment gives him greater freedom of movement, and his rigour means that he can take refuge inside the protective framework of the law. The rational individual obviously establishes bonds, but he also remains in control and the bonds are therefore revocable. Love, in contrast, creates bonds that can never be broken as it grows stronger, and this can lead to the loss of the most personal elements of our individual autonomy.

A COMMUNITY BASED ON LOVE

The type of bond that is created varies, depending on whether it is forged by passion or by universal love, and depending on the historical context. For centuries, *agape* dreamed of creating a new holism. Peter Brown (1988), for instance, describes how the pagans were greatly impressed by the first radical sects; they were struck by their ability to establish a generalized friendship that bound together all the members of the community in ways that were both intimate and chaste. The dream lasted for a long time. Think, for instance, of the fourteenth-century *Fioretti* (Francis of Assisi 1959 [1386]). This is a literary text (short and would-be-edifying stories that enjoyed great popularity) that refers to facts whose historical reality is open to challenge. But it is its moral implications that are really important. Published after the death of St Francis of Assisi, the *Fioretti* was a sort of programme for a minority group of radical Franciscans. The general idea was to do everything possible to repress personal desires and to promote a cult of self-sacrifice – and, through that self-sacrifice, to encourage 'others to turn to love' (Boltanski 1990: 189). This love could forge community bonds that were all the stronger in that it was generous, had no ulterior motives and could even be unthinking and silent. Absolute self-sacrifice was all that mattered, and it was so attractive that its influence spread and eventually caused the group to fuse into a single being.

If it was to have this effect, pure love had to function as a purely emotional abstraction. Most Franciscans, and St Francis himself, in fact took a different view. Giving to the poor was, they observed, not enough; how their gifts were received and used was just as important. They had noticed that some of the poor who received gifts were just as greedy as the rich. They had also noticed that some needs were essential, whilst others were not. And they noticed, finally, that if gifts were to be given on a broader scale, it would be necessary to handle money, and that they therefore had to define the relationship between gifts and money. Giacomo Todeschini (2008 [2004]) supplies a very convincing analysis of the paradoxes involved in this. He demonstrates that the desire to make a precise analysis resulted in the development of intellectual tools and an economic language that played an essential role in the future development of a market economy. The Franciscans were trying to see how disinterested love could create a fairer, more effective and more realistic basis for the social bond, but they accelerated the process that made money its central regulator.

Did this mean that a love that aspired to being the basis of a human community had to ignore concrete realities? Although the fourteenth-century Jesuit Pierre de Jean Olivi did not have a direct answer to that question, he did establish a typology of possible forms of holism (Boureau 2005). He made, for instance, a distinction between the secret communities of the chosen, who were on the path leading to mystical perfection, and communities of citizens who thought it was their duty to work for the common good in society as it was, even if that meant becoming involved in commodity exchanges. Sadly – and as we have seen, and as we will see once more – love quickly loses its soul when it decides to involve itself in the affairs of this world. And that is, in part, why it is so mysterious: it is always elsewhere.

Romeo Can Never Again be Romeo

Ever since the dawn of time, passion has been a vector for personal emancipation, and an 'experiment in self-assertion' that defies both the social order (Barrère and Martuccelli 2009: 250) and the desires of families who attempt to lay down the law. And, for a long time, this was a major theme for plays and novels all over Europe: love laughed at institutions, and Romeo and Juliet listened only to their hearts. In holistic societies in which the individual is caught up in moral and social structures that tell him or her which road to take, passion can distract him or her from that implacable destiny and open up the roads that lead to freedom and personal fulfilment. Reason, conversely, was still seen as something that structured the world-order (even though Reason too was quietly beginning to become emancipated). In today's society, it is precisely the opposite: individual rationality openly cuts individuals off from the world around them, whilst love binds them to the people or the things they love. Everything has been turned upside down. Romeo can never again be Romeo. He may well experience mad passions, but they no longer have anything to do with freedom. Passion now means commitment, and the more violent the passion, the greater the commitment. And it is the commitment that is frightening. We no longer live in a holistic society, and the passions no longer face any obstacles: there is no danger of a cruel conflict with one's family and with an institution (which means that Shakespeare would have nothing to write about).

It is commitment that causes all the problems: it might restrict our individual autonomy. Even love at first sight is going out of fashion. We may well dream of it (Schurmans and Dominicé 1997), but we all think twice about falling in love. Especially if we have already been let down. Love at first sight is, by definition, irresistible and the idea of being plunged into the madness of a liaison (in the 'binding' sense) is as frightening as it is appealing. We would prefer love to be something that happens in a flash. A flash (the word is very fashionable) can be intense and exciting but, unlike love at first sight, it does not suggest the idea of an ever-lasting commitment. It happens very quickly. It is dazzling, and there can be more than one flash. The electricity of love now appears to us in a different form, and this explains why the flashes have become much more frequent: they can happen anywhere, and especially on public transport and in public places where we fleetingly bump into or even rub up against people we do not know. Why public transport? For the very good reason that what we are really afraid of is suffocation, of being unable to express our personal lives. Flashes are therefore triggered more easily when we come into fleeting contact with others. And they have given rise to the new and increasingly popular activity of posting what we might call post-flash personal ads. Here is an example taken from a specialist website:

> *Beautiful stranger on the Métro, Friday, 9.45–9.50,*
> *heading to Boulogne*
> *Hello, beautiful.*
> *I was sitting in the seat in front of you this morning.*
> *You were scribbling something on a piece of paper, and then*
> *you got off the métro at Porte d'Auteuil . . . You smiled*
> *at me as you walked along the platform.*
> *I would love to see you again.*
> *David*

It would obviously be a very different story if the man who placed the advert got a reply. But it strikes me that many of these ads are a little too vague, and do not give enough detail for anyone to recognize themselves. It is as though the flash itself was all that mattered.

'A Man Is Not a Pot of Yoghurt'

Love now faces a new challenge: the lonely individual has to become attached to someone, but in a different way. Before that can happen, we have to construct a new model of the individual. This inevitably involves an element of schizophrenia, and that gets worse once the 'rational individual' model begins to impinge upon our private lives. This is rarely the case when it comes to relations with children, which are still governed by an unconditional commitment. When it comes to couples, however, both partners tend increasingly to use the critical assessment techniques associated with the rational individual model. This usually takes the form of an exercise in book-keeping: we secretly list our partner's bad points . . . and go on doing so until a sudden crisis brings the critical vision to the fore (Kaufmann 2009 [2007]). The rational individual model is even beginning to be used to determine our initial choice of partner, especially on on-line dating sites. We have here an absolute contradiction, something that is completely impossible. We cannot establish bonds if we evaluate people on a rational basis. Those who surf the net do not always realize this: it is only when they reach the commitment stage that the penny drops, and commitment becomes infinitely more difficult if their first exchanges were evaluated on a rational basis. We simply cannot commit ourselves unless we are in love, and unless we undergo a change of identity. Rational thought cuts us off from the world and makes us fall back on our own points of reference. In our dreams, we will always be the way we are now. We have an easy conscience and assume that we can simply introduce someone else into our lives. Now, that is quite impossible. There can be no commitment unless we change. That has to be a profound change, not just in our day-to-day habits, but deep down inside us (Berger and Kellner 1964). The problem with the internet is that it makes us think just the opposite, at least when we begin to use it.

Take the example of women. Initially somewhat dubious about it, they are becoming increasingly interested in on-line dating. With only one click, they can see a whole procession of men. Nice, smiling men who are available and who show off their male attributes as they pose in swimming trunks or in their bikers' leathers. With just one click a woman can choose any one of them. Welcome to the consumerist illusion that would have us believe that a woman can choose a man as easily as she can choose a pot of yoghurt in a hypermarket. But that is not how love works: it cannot be reduced to rational thought, and still less can it be reduced to consumerism. A man is not a pot of yoghurt, and a woman cannot just introduce a man into her life and expect that nothing will change as a result. On the contrary: he will turn her life upside down. She will never be the same again, and nor will he. Meeting someone and falling in love with them metamorphoses both their identities. That is what is so irresistibly attractive – and so frightening – about it.

The illusion is very powerful to begin with. For a woman who is comfortably sitting at home, knowing that she can go on-line is an incomparable source of mental reassurance. One click is all it takes to log on, and another click is all it takes to log off. With one click, she can look at a 'profile', and with another click she can move on to another one. By clicking she can send an e-mail, and by not clicking she doesn't even reply to the reply. A surfer armed with a mouse imagines herself to be in complete control of her social contacts. The early stages are exciting. The usual obstacles seem to have vanished, and a world of infinite possibilities opens up. She is as spoilt for choice as a child who has been let loose in a sweet shop.

Sadly, the magic soon fades when a real decision has to be made. Seeing so many men on offer was exciting to begin with, but it quickly becomes mentally exhausting. Too much is too much, and too much choice makes it impossible to choose. Christelle, or 'Canalchris' as she calls herself, feels that her head is spinning. 'In any case, they're all the same when you look at their details. Charming, sporty, honest, generous, funny, "no mind games", good looking, sensual . . . They might as well guarantee you'll be on cloud nine. Everyone's a winner! Oh, come on!' (Kaufmann 2008a [1999]: 118; the comments from 'Canalchris' are taken from her blog). So she decides to define what she is looking for in greater detail. Half Prince Charming, half a clone of herself. Leisure activities, affinities: the idea is to find someone who is like her, which is the basic principle behind on-line contacts. But 'someone like her' really means someone who will leave everything unchanged, who won't turn her life upside down, who will not change its rhythm, and who will not upset her little habits. She is looking for a pot of yoghurt and not for a man. And that makes commitment all the more difficult.

Despite everything, we do forget about ourselves and we do allow ourselves to be carried away by our emotions, thanks to a subtle art that might be called the new art of love. The important thing is that love goes on resisting the imperialism of the 'calculating individual' model: there can be no conjugal commitment without love, and that is a reassuring thought. And perhaps love has not abandoned its other, broader ambitions. Its bid to structure the individualization of society may have ended in failure, but love has not given up the idea of extending its empire. It tried to do so in two different ways. Initially, or just after it was marginalized by the internet, there was a vogue for great revolutionary ideas and flamboyant utopias that were as radical as they were hopeless. They all ended in failure, but some of the ideas behind them have had a great influence on our period, which has seen an unexpected revival of interest in love as it begins to try to outflank the calculating individual.

But we need to look first at love's revolutionaries.

3

Love's Revolutionaries

BENEVOLENCE AND VIRTUE

Before it was reduced to meaning cold, calculating self-interest, Enlightenment Reason thought of itself as something warmer than that. In a sense, the artisans of the Enlightenment dreamed of creating a new holism and of using Reason to produce a society that was not just more enlightened but also more tolerant and fairer. The Enlightenment agenda initially associated these moral principles with the idea of Reason. Although they were still thinking in Christian terms, the philosophers of the Enlightenment were in fact secularizing society. In order to do that, a whole series of notions had to be remodelled and translated into a new language. The grandiose concept of Reason had set out on the long journey that would lead to the law on which democracy is based and to the rights of man, which held out the prospect of a universal magnanimity. Sadly, the same journey also led to the small-mindedness of the calculating individual. The political world invented the tools that would allow it to become autonomous from religion (Gauchet 1997 [1985]). Love, in the meantime, was diverted into the private sphere, where it acted mainly as a source of consolation.

Love as a whole did not suffer that fate, however. Before economic mathematics succeeded in regulating the world, it was widely believed that the social bond could be based upon a combination of moral feelings and Reason. These were virtuous, generous and benevolent feelings. What was to be done? It did not look that complicated: surely translating the Christian *agape* into a new and secular benevolence would be enough? The Enlightenment was based upon the conviction that Good could be associated with Reason, and it was only in the nineteenth and twentieth centuries that it gave way to the belief that technological progress was synonymous with moral progress, and could make the planet's peoples happy.

At this stage, the market economy was still a marginal phenomenon, but some thinkers were already worried by the mediocrity of the passions it inspired, as compared with the greatness of universal benevolence. Rousseau, a critique of consumer society *avant la lettre*, railed against the attractions of pathetic 'knick-knacks' (cited Hirschman 1983: 88). With the Revolution at its height, Robespierre adopted Rousseau's thesis in his attacks on those who had turned to looting shops; in his view, the people's energies should be redirected into republican virtues. Charles Taylor explains why Rousseau's theses were so important to the French Revolution: moral feeling played a central role in it. The idea of justice was obviously important, but so too was the idea of virtue. It was hoped that 'the benevolence latent in virtuous men' (Taylor 1989: 387) would bring about a world-wide revolution. Similar millenarian expectations could be observed in England and Germany. Rationally-based principles, social justice and individual emancipation would, it was widely believed, promote good and universal feelings that would help a new humanity to emerge. The idea of a secular *agape* was central to the democratic and republican revolutions that would turn Europe upside-down.

A BLEEDING HEART

Let me dwell on this revolutionary episode for a moment, as it is an important moment in the political history of love. The Enlightenment gave rise to the idea that a feeling of universal benevolence could spring from Reason and forge the social bond. There was also a tendency to mythologize and idealize the people. The aristocracy was debauched and the powerful were tyrannical, but the people were seen as the perfect image of purity, sincerity and all that was natural, and identified with the 'noble savage' of the New World and with Europe's peasantry. Bucolic paintings and fairy tales turned shepherds into icons of the truth about love, and their harsh living conditions were simply overlooked. Once upon a time there was a prince, and a shepherdess . . . The regenerative purity of private love was associated with the much broader regeneration of society as a whole. Richardson in England, Gellert in Germany and Goldoni in Italy 'all appealed to the virtue of the people in a bid to save love and the nation' (Bologne 1998: 113). The effervescence of the Revolution obviously heightened these emotionally based moral expectations. For better, to begin with – and then, alas, for worse.

Everything got off to a fairly good start. The Declaration of the Rights of Man was seen as a civilizing process that gave the people direct access to politics (Wahnich 2008). This development unleashed a new fervour and enthusiasm, and those emotions were all the more effective at binding the people together in that their origins were religious, as was obvious from the secular high masses celebrated by the Revolution. Sophie Wahnich (2008) stresses that this enthusiasm was at its greatest in the revolutionary clubs, where the combination of passion and physical proximity really did fuse the group. Contemporary observers used electrical metaphors (a sort of public version of the thunderbolt metaphor that describes love at first sight) to describe this communion, and shared emotion did as much as intellectual exchanges to rapidly promote a total communion. A clash of opinions, in contrast, is always likely to be divisive. When they abandoned the Enlightenment ideal of mutual benevolence, these emotional crowds began to be swayed by passion, which is a very different form of love. Only passion can generate the level of electricity that causes a group to fuse together; *agape* never manifests itself in this way. Being universal, *agape* sees the world as it is, and it sees the world as a whole,[1] whereas passion is always individual – which is what gives it its emotional power. Passion creates a counter-world, and it therefore creates divisions. The ambiguity of these revolutionary

[1] Robespierre did, however, point out that benevolence does have its limitations. It speaks to 'the entire human race, minus the tyrants and their accomplices' (Wahnich 2008: 475).

feelings masked the conflict between two types of love. The inevitable happened, and universal virtues were swamped by partisan passions.

In the early stages of the Revolution, everyone made a huge effort to ensure that mutual benevolence held back the flood of individual passions and prevented intellectual debates from becoming physically violent. *L'Ami des citoyens* describes how, when Brissot and Robespierre clashed over the issue of war, the Jacobin Club organized a 'touching reconciliation scene'. The political enemies flung themselves into each others' arms and hugged one another before an assembly that was 'moved to tears' (cited Wahnich 2008: 121). It is interesting to note that it is still common for rivals to embrace one another in the contemporary political world: a ritual that takes its points of reference from private love is used to ward off potential conflicts. The embrace itself is chaste, but the gesture is borrowed from the language of lovers. Love circulates in surprising ways between its opposites, and between the very different private and public spaces in which it manifests itself.

Unfortunately, embraces cannot overcome all differences of opinion. One difficult question, in particular, gave rise to debates between the revolutionaries. The new laws were certainly magnificent and egalitarian, but did they apply to those who subverted them by appealing to the virtues of the people? Surely moral feelings that emanated from Reason and found natural expression through the voice of the people transcended the law? Until 1792, most people had a very clear answer to that question: just men and benevolent feelings, and not the law, should rule the world. Witness the following motion (cited Wahnich 2008: 373): 'The longer our mores retain the degree of purity and gentleness that always recalls a love of humanity and of virtue, the more they will protect and guarantee civil liberties. . . . Laws alone cannot have a protective influence unless these gentle mores become more common, or without this invigorating sensitivity that magnifies men's affections.' Universal love was the ultimate guarantee.

This ideal was shipwrecked on the inevitable differences of opinion and the passions that they unleashed. When, on 20 June 1792, 8,000 demonstrators burst into the Assemblée in a bid to force the *députés* to endorse their petition, the prevailing atmosphere was still one of fraternal humanity. There were women and children present and they danced to the drums and music as though they had come for a huge picnic on the Champ-de-Mars. But the group that entered the chamber to the applause of some *députés* was also carrying all kinds of weapons. The way the legislators felt about popular passions that could not always be kept under control was about to change. Some were especially shocked by one detail: a bleeding heart brandished at the point of a lance and bearing the legend 'heart of an aristocrat'. It was in fact the heart of a calf, but it was also a sign of the terrible blood-letting that was to come. Before long, heads were being cut off in the name of virtue. The bleeding heart also indicated that some very different sensibilities were at work. The sight of such a thing inside the chamber that was supposed to defend the law was offensive to many *députés*, including some who supported the petitioners. The need for a public force that had the backing of the law and that could repress anarchic outbursts of popular rage was becoming obvious. They would have to be repressed at the expense of the human virtues that were supposed to rule the world. And they would have to be repressed in the name of 'honest men'. La Fayette demanded that the 'seditionaries' of 20 June be punished as though they were criminals. He had already unhesitatingly given the order to shoot those who were picnicking on the Champ-de-Mars. The modern state was being established. It was clearly based on a strict interpretation of the law, took no notice of expressions of the emotions, and did not care if they were universally benevolent or impassioned.

A passionate love of the group to which one belongs all too easily turns into a hatred of enemy groups. This is as true of the Jacobin Terror as it is of the various nationalisms of the twentieth century and of the religious fundamentalism of the twenty-first. 'Once again, men failed in their bid for happiness' (De Planhol 1921: 207). Love had proved to have its limitations as a political principle.

STENDHAL: THE DISAPPOINTMENTS OF AMERICA

Speaking of La Fayette, let me invite you on a short trip to America. We will be in very good company, as we will be with Stendhal, who was the great novelist of the passions. He will be our guide, and he will help us to understand how a public failure had a considerable impact on our private loves.

Although Stendhal was still a child in 1792, he came from a family of Jacobins and was therefore actively involved in public life. It should also be remembered that, at the time, 'the French Revolution and the American Revolution were one and the same' (Crouzet 2008: 85). Stendhal, who had immediately rallied to La Fayette, followed the political upheavals that were taking place in the New World with great interest. He 'immediately felt himself to be American' (Crouzet 2008: 85). European intellectuals had projected onto America the hope that a benevolent Reason would be embodied in the Republic. What had ended in failure on the Old Continent might still end in success on the other side of the Atlantic. Stendhal was not, and never would be, lukewarm when it came to emotional matters, and his correspondence reveals the extent to which he was seduced – blinded, even – by the American Revolution, and the intoxicating happiness of seeing the forces of human intelligence. His enthusiasm suddenly faded somewhere between 1820 and 1830, and liberal opinion in Europe turned against developments in America at the same time.

So what happened? Stendhal followed developments very carefully, and he was bitterly disappointed. He had nothing against money in personal terms, and had even thought briefly of becoming a banker in Marseille. He was, on the other hand, disgusted at the idea that mean self-interest might interfere with the great ideas that had been applied to the evolution of humanity. And that is precisely what was happening in America, where, more so than anywhere else, the rational individual model had been reduced to the calculating individual model very quickly and very effectively. The outcome was a society that simply horrified him: 'The vulgarity of pleasures, the monotony of working life, the hegemony of economic and technological values, the worship of money and material well-being, the pointless idolatry' (cited Crouzet 2008: 134). He dreamed of something very different. He dreamed of creative energy and of the love of beauty, but 'Economics has killed aesthetics and this prosaic life has destroyed souls' (cited Crouzet 2008: 173). Italy now took the place of America in his mind, or rather his heart. Italy did not provide a political model, but it did inspire passion. His disappointed love for the United States led him to rage against Americans, whom he accused of being quite incapable of experiencing passionate love: 'There is such a *habit of reason* in the United States that the crystallization of love there has become impossible . . . they have no life left with which to enjoy' (Stendhal 1975 [1822]: 164). In America, 'men are motivated by only three things: money, freedom and God' (cited Crouzet 2008: 19).

Struck by the bleakness of American society, Stendhal began to have his doubts about Reason. It was Reason that had cut people off from their environment, and it became even more hateful when it was reduced to meaning utilitarian calculation. But in Europe, the liberal left that had emerged from the Enlightenment was still supporting the American experiment and developing an industrialist ideology of progress. Stendhal therefore had to change his political vision, as he could not endorse that view of progress. He believed, on the contrary, that man had to rediscover the enthusiasm that brought colour into the world and warmth into humanity. In more general terms, the industrialism of progress inspired the whole romantic reaction and radicalized its political tonality. It adopted an anti-Enlightenment stance, and rejected the heritage of the Enlightenment and its coldness in favour of the passions. Several hundred years after courtly love and the *Tristan* romance, a very broad movement once again tried to invoke love in order to change the world. But the situation was no longer the same. The 'calculating individual' model was already at work, and it was redefining the rules of the game. Romanticism was a desperate form of resistance, and that goes some way to explaining why it could be at once so despairing and so absolute. It was, so to speak, the final act of resistance before money took complete control.

THE PINK AND THE BLACK

Although he was carried away by the fashion for romanticism, Stendhal was not exactly the typical romantic. He has been described as 'an ambiguous romantic' (Crouzet 1965: 19) who had little time for pessimism and who dreamed of passions that could bring him joy. When he speaks of courtly love, for instance, he evokes refined arts imbued with 'love, grace and gaiety' (Stendhal 1975 [1822]: 169) but he has nothing to say about the mystical heritage of the gloomy Cathars. And yet the tormented passions that emerged in reaction to the way early industrial society impoverished life worked just as they had done in the age of courtly love: there were two sides to romanticism. The trend did not begin with Stendhal or with the French romantics. Like courtly love, which eventually took the form of poems and songs, French romanticism simply adopted the more stylized aspects of something that already existed. A few years earlier, romanticism had launched an infinitely more radical programme, especially in Germany. It was based upon a mystical vision, and it was that vision that gave it its strength and impetus: 'To extol the death undergone deliberately for the sake of love and in order to be absorbed into the divine – such was the deep religious purpose of the new Albigensian heresy called German romanticism' (Rougemont 1983 [1940]: 219). As in the story of Tristan and Isolde – and it is no accident that Wagner should have picked it up – the underlying idea was that of a total passion that offered the individual a subjectivity that was 'so autonomous as to be almost divine' (Girard 2004 [1961]: 43). That subjectivity allowed the individual to invent a new world that was dreamlike and poetic, and that had nothing in common with the petty-mindedness of bureaucrats and bankers. Unfortunately, and as in the case of Tristan, creating that world meant rejecting the existing world. This counter-world was painted in dark, sad colours. It existed elsewhere, was both sombre and mysterious, and relished the sweet pain of a nostalgic dream. The idea of death was never far away, and that heightened the emotions still further. Emotion was the hidden treasure and the Holy Grail. Our emotional impulses and the excitement of seeing spirituality and sensuality merge into one allows us to discover that our truth lies within us. Emotion takes us into the strange plenitude of a harmonious world, and the melancholy that underpins our intuition tells us that this harmony is nothing but a dream. The individual is a lonely demiurge who, in a statement of excitement that is similar to the madness of the poets, arrives at the paradoxical conclusion that 'the individual is nothing' and that 'the whole exists in its own right' (Senancour 1799: 30).

Once again, great passion therefore leads to sadness, and this infinite sadness is terrifyingly close to death. The ultimate experiment in radical romanticism, which did, alas, lead to real deaths (there was a wave of suicides as young men sought to imitate

Goethe's melancholic hero Werther), resulted in something that in many respects now exists in contradictory forms. Just as courtly love ended with poems that softened our mores, romanticism became infinitely gentle. Curiously enough, it is because the black was so intensely black that romanticism could later reappear in the pastel colours typical of modern-day 'romanticism', and still have the same effects.

DARKNESS AND LIGHT

Radical romanticism was such a sublime dream of loving perfection that it could never become a reality, and it never sought to become a reality. Its energy was in fact the product of a lack: the emotion that impelled the individual to pursue a goal that could never be attained was all that mattered. Romanticism was a 'longing for infinity' (Bologne 1998: 137). And insofar as it implied a political project, it was always doomed to failure. I say 'political project' because romanticism saw love between two people (meaning, of course, true love) as a model for the restructuring of society as a whole, the basic idea being that sentimentality could be part of an all-encompassing totality. Enlightenment Reason, in contrast, drove people apart, divided them and made them emotionally cold. The romantic idea was obviously fine in itself, but it remained very vague and did not have a programme that could actually be implemented. And the political heritage of romanticism was, sadly, often reactionary, if not bloodthirsty, and had very little to do with the original idea.

In a period characterized by the individualization of society, romanticism offered a vision that rejected the self-interest that really was taking control of an increasingly active market economy (Löwy and Sayre 1992). The rational-calculating individual model needed a concrete support if it was to go on developing, and it found that support in money. The romantic individual also had a very real support in the form of passionate love. This explains why the spiritual, philosophical or political undertones were not always obvious: love was everywhere. Radical romanticism gave the impression that it dealt only with sentimental and private issues, but they were just the raw materials for its most grandiose ambitions, 'which bordered on the "supernatural" ' (de Planhol

1921: 266). It failed to realize its ambitions, but that was not the end for radical romanticism: it still had the private passions.[2] Political romanticism was a historical phenomenon that lasted for only a short time, but its emotional implications were far-reaching. Much the same thing had already happened with courtly love, the difference being that we are the direct heirs to romanticism, as is obvious from the way we talk of love. The growing emphasis on pure sentimentality therefore requires careful study. Many of the words and gestures that we still associate with love relate to what happened when romanticism turned darkness into light.

I have mentioned romanticism's dark colours, and it did at times display a certain fondness for graveyards, but things are in fact a little more complicated than that. Like love itself, romanticism was characterized by an interplay between opposites. It was deeply personal and highly subjective, but it wanted to dissolve the self into a totality. It was a poetically and abstractly spiritual élan, but it fed on very physical sensations. It was imbued with melancholy and even pain, but it perfected the art of secretly finding pleasure in tears (and what could be more beautiful than a broken heart?). And I could go on: it is these contrasting dualities that gave romanticism its strength, and that is what has allowed it to survive – in different form – until today. But there was always a gleam of light somewhere in the darkness. That is why the inversion was so spectacular: it was not really an inversion after all. It is quite simple: as one face of romanticism disappeared, the other appeared. When the philosophical and political project ended in failure, personal passions took centre-stage. The dark colours were products of the mystical side of the romantic adventure, which followed a typically Manichean schema. They therefore faded when the spiritual impulse died. The same thing happened with courtly love, but there was one difference. The Cathar religion had always stayed in the background and had simply influenced the movement from behind the scenes. Before it became little more than a behavioural stance characterized by a mood and its strength of feeling, romanticism was always its own

---

[2] Romanticism also bequeathed us the vague but very influential image that still depicts the artist as a rebel subject who creates a world of his own (Heinich 1991, 1996). Artistic creation has a lot in common with romantic passion, which also creates a counter-world.

religion. The same word was used to describe two very different realities, but there was a common thread to all the facets of romanticism.

The common thread is passion. Passion was the 'revolutionary' movement (Alberoni 1994) that created a counter-world and rejected the old world. 'Insofar as it is a passion, love really does build a "world" for two' (Genard 1995: 75). For radical romanticism, the absolute, perfect world was inevitably an unreal world that existed only because of the emotional impulse that wrested it away from a prosaic reality. It invented a dream world of emotions that could not exist in the real world. The next episode in the story is about how romanticism came to terms with some aspects of the real world. Although it still rejected prosaic reality, it no longer went in pursuit of an unreal absolute; it wanted to create a world that could find a place where it could have a real existence. It was still a little world, and it was still poetic and sentimental, but it really did exist somewhere in the real world. Such was the new challenge offered by these new forms of passion, which owed its strength to the romanticism of old. It went in search of life, but it could not have done so without the darkness.

BACK TO REALITY

Romanticism failed as a political project because it had no practical programme (vague attempts to implement it resulted in disasters such as the excesses of fanatical nationalism). It was forced to abandon its dream because it had been subjected to criticisms – sometimes violent but more often mocking – in the name of reality. Its vaporous complaints were laughed out of court. Love needed something it could get hold of.

All over Europe, theologians, philosophers and doctors were putting this radical romanticism in the dock. Its mad passions posed a threat to the new bourgeois order and did not lead to anything worthwhile. To hell with these medieval mists and this suicidal melancholy! Love had to get back in touch with ordinary life. The new science of alienism decreed, with all the authority of medical science, that the madness of love was madness, pure and simple, and that love sickness was just another sickness. And the sick had to be treated. Now that the torments of romanticism were over, good society dreamed of getting back to normal. The writers were not so sure about this. They were happy to criticize romanticism's excesses, but they were reluctant to sacrifice passion's creative energy. If your name was Emma, I would spend a lot of time telling you about Flaubert. And even though you are not called Emma, I will say a little about Flaubert because both his life and his work are good illustrations of this development. Louise was sitting for a sculptor when Gustave first met her, and he was immediately dazzled by her beauty. Louise, a poet who had experienced mad passion, was a true romantic. At the time, Gustave prided himself on feeling the same impulses and he played at being a romantic, but soon tired of the game. There was more to life than this, he said to himself, thinking mainly of his literary work. Passions that were too violent and too complete suffocated him, and he wanted to be able to breathe. 'Spare me! You are making me giddy with your love', he wrote.[3] Romanticism had to know its own limitations and get back to the real world. 'I am tired of grand passions, exalted feelings, mad love and howling despair.'[4] When Louise refused to come down from the heights of sentimentality, Flaubert lost his temper and became even more negative. 'In my view, love is not and must not be the most important thing in life; it has to remain in the background.'[5] Playing at being a romantic was all very well, but he was not prepared to let romanticism take over his whole life. Unlike Emma Bovary, he was not going to be taken in by love's illusions; pure romanticism came at too high a price. Flaubert therefore attempted to introduce some emotional truths into the rich, complex reality of life. He was not the only one to do so, and subsequent literature was influenced by a new realism.

French literature did not, however, forget about Stendhal, precisely because he was a more ambiguous romantic. He wanted to experience the emotional impulses that transcended the narrow confines of the ordinary world, but not their morbidity, and not their disastrous outcome. To put it very simply, Stendhal wanted to experience a passion that could be happy, even joyous. That is what makes him a pioneer. He often looks like a pessimist, but

[3] Letter of 13 September 1846 to Louise Collet.
[4] Letter of December 1846 to Louise Collet.
[5] Letter of 30 April 1847 to Louise Collet.

that is because he did not succeed in discovering the alchemy that creates happy passions: either it was a dream that could not exist in the real world, or it melted away when it came into contact with reality. And he could not discover passion's alchemy because the times were not ripe for it. René Girard underlines Stendhal's failure, but sees it as a failure on the part of passion itself ('Stendhal's impotence is revealing. The creature of passion is a creature from the past, and is narrowly, superstitiously religious' (Girard 2004 [1961]: 83)). Now, that is a feature of mystical passion, and it can exist in other forms of passion too. Stendhal was not wrong to go in search of it. He was not a man who looked to the past. On the contrary, he was an innovator. It took society 100 years to begin to come to terms with the new idea of happy passions and, before that could happen, romanticism had to undergo several mutations.

Nikolas Luhmann points out that romanticism initially appealed only to the literary elite, and its influence was slow to spread, even in diluted form (Luhmann 1990 [1984]). He is not mistaken. But that must not be allowed to conceal a fact that had a considerable impact. Edward Shorter notes that, throughout the nineteenth century, it was the reference to romantic love (in a diluted form, admittedly) that gradually allowed mutual affection to govern the individual's choice of partner, rather than the institutional weight of families or of tradition. Individualistic modernity made use of the ideals of romanticism to establish the undisputed norm for the behaviour of all young people who were looking for a partner (see Shorter 1975: 181ff.).

LOVE IN UTOPIA

The romantic impulse was a reaction against the coldness of Reason. At roughly the same time, another protest movement raised the banner of love. Whereas the romantics tended to be artists and poets, the utopians were more likely to be organizers and political activists, but both parties used dreams as weapons. Both tried to fight the cold indifference of the world by appealing to the emotions, and tried to overcome factionalism in a bid to create harmony. Harmony is one of Fourier's key words. He argues the case for a situation that would encourage 'the release

of all the passions' (Fourier 1941 [1808]: 118), as opposed to the
deadly 'counter-passion' of egotism, which he describes as a miserable attitude that traps us into pathetic little calculations. The
passions would allow man to reveal all that is best within him,
and to be more receptive to others. His phalansteries were designed
to make this possible.

The word 'utopia' has a long history that can be traced back
to the English writer Thomas More, who published his *Utopia* in
1516. In it, he describes his dream of a different type of society
that rejected the grasping mentality encouraged by monetary
exchanges. His utopia is based upon the principle of 'communism
minus money' (More 2003 [1516]: 113). Even at this stage, money
was seen as the enemy. That idea would be taken up by the utopians who followed in More's footsteps. As their plans for alternatives to monetary regulation became more concrete, they came to
attach more and more importance to love. Take the eccentric and
relatively unknown François Boissel. Three months before the
outbreak of the French Revolution, the politically active Boissel,
who was the Vice-President of the Jacobin Club, was drawing
up imaginary plans for a possible world. Based on the values of
what we would now describe as solidarity, feminism and environ-
mentalism, he called for the abolition of private property, religion
and marriage. Nothing more and nothing less. Women would
play the central role in Boissel's utopia, which was to be based on
love. Its goal was 'to make us happy by making one another
happy' (Boissel 2007 [1789]: 84). But what did he mean by love
when he spoke of discovering happiness? This is where the utopians began to have their differences. Some opted for mutual benevolence, and some for the passions, including the most carnal
passions.

Auguste Comte, for example, argued the case for universal
values. Comte is not usually regarded as a utopian, and tends to
be seen as a very serious, if not austere, scholar. And yet he too
had his utopia, and it too was based on love. At the scientific level,
Comte introduced ideas of great importance that are still essential
today, especially in epistemology. His contributions to any discussion of love, on the other hand, are debatable, to say the least.
Take, for instance, the preposterous idea of doing away with sensuality and voluptuousness! In his bid to develop his 'religion of

humanity', he insisted that marriage must be as chaste as possible, and argued that the instincts should be content with a 'very moderate' satisfaction (Comte 1874 [1852]: 286). But his utopianism went much further than this. Comte was a visionary when it came to technology, but his vision of human relations was terrifying. He even dreamed of new reproductive methods that would allow us to do away with sexuality. 'That is why I came to describe the utopia of the Virgin-Mother as a synthetic précis of positive religion' (Comte 1851: vol. IV, 168). The Virgin-Mother ... doesn't that remind you of something? Yes, courtly love. Auguste Comte did not simply want to base his system on a secular *agape*. He was also thinking of more personal feelings. But those feelings were so lofty and ethereal that his utopia wanted to have nothing to do with the problems created by real bodies. Not surprisingly, his love-based programme did not pull in the crowds. We have no cause to complain about that.

Charles Fourier had more success. He too believed that the harmonious social bond had to be based upon *agape*. '*Unitéisme* refers to the individual's propensity to reconcile his happiness with that of those around him, and the human race, which is now so hateful, can display the same propensity. *Unitéisme* means boundless philanthropy and universal benevolence' (Fourier 1941 [1808]: 116). This general virtue was, however, no more than the starting point that would encourage the art of discovering talents by liberating all kinds of passion – including the most voluptuous passions. Orgies should be organized, but there would be nothing vulgar about them: the goal was to 'exalt souls' and to use 'an excess of well-being' to strive for 'generalized friendship' and 'transcendent love' (Fourier 2003 [1816]: 243). Women, in particular, had put marriage out of their minds, as it both trapped and humiliated them. In the ideal society, women would have four categories of partner, each playing a different role in their games of love (like many utopians, Fourier took a pedantic delight in quantifying his programmes). During the great courtly feasts presided over by a 'Matron-Superior', women would choose their partners for the night. The unfortunate men who were not chosen were regarded as wounded, and there were special guilds to take care of their physical needs. The lucky suitor who was rewarded by his beloved, in contrast, was awarded the sought-after title of 'troubadour'. Fourier derived many of his points of reference from courtly love, but he did not share Comte's mystical ideals. He was interested in its voluptuousness, its douceur, its gallantry, and especially the strange alchemy that allowed the liveliest passions to become part of a universal benevolence.

LOVE CANNOT BE GOVERNED BY DECREE

The great love-based utopias of people like Fourier emerged at a particular moment in history. Society had abandoned the religious holism that had once provided it with a moral framework, but Reason's attempts to enlighten the world had ended in failure. Reason had been replaced by its pale imitation, and the calculating individual had become the pivot around which society was reorganized. Freedom came at a price: life seemed to offer few prospects, rather as though everything was now grounded in the base materiality of the world, and that did not bring out the best in human beings.

Romanticism had already rebelled against this gloomy prospect in the name of an individual who aspired to being a god. The utopians also began by excoriating society, but they went in a different direction. The calculating individual around whom the whole of society revolved had yet to become the dominant model. In what now looks like a historical interlude, it was believed that society could respond to vast institutional programmes that gave the impression that a secular religion could take the place of the old religion, and that a collective morality and rules for a collective life would be elaborated. The dream of a new holism, which was already beginning to look archaic, was vital to utopianism, and that holism was, of course, based upon love. But in an age in which the individual was emerging as the dominant figure, it was only within sects that were cut off from the rest of society that holism could flourish. And that is what happened.

Unlike romanticism, the great utopias had little influence on subsequent forms of love (the new communities that were established in May '68 even forgot that they had ever existed). They ended in total failure, which only goes to prove that no decree can ensure that it is love and not money that regulates the social bond. There were, however, a lot of lessons to be learned from these failures. Love has probably always dreamed of ruling the world. The lessons of the past might, then, prove useful.

But let me first say a word about Fourier. Whilst he does have his good side (a loathing of egotism, a sincere desire to spread happiness, and some ideas about women's emancipation that were shared by few of his contemporaries), he also has a less appealing side. His prescriptions are incredibly bureaucratic and pedantic. In the earthly paradise he wanted to create, everything is organized down to the last detail. Even pleasures are listed, classified and quantified. The status of lovers is dissected with a diabolical precision. The 'horned world' (of cuckolds), for instance, is divided into numerous categories: 'The complete table consists of sixty-four species, which are gradually divided into classes, orders and genera ranging from "budding cuckold" to "posthumous cuckold" ' (Fourier 1941 [1808]: 188). We now find all these lists and classifications irresistibly funny, but Fournier was not joking. In his plans for the future, the number and type of meals was predetermined. There were rules dictating what should be worn for every ritual, and which forms of erotic behaviour were appropriate for every occasion. There was even a 'Minister for Loving Relationships', namely the above-mentioned 'Matron-Superior', who was supplied with lists of the 'secret' unions that had been formed on the night of the courtly feast. The beautiful utopian dream turned into a dictatorial farce. Unfortunately, that lesson does not only apply to Fourier's utopia. Many love stories still get off to a good start and end badly, and what is true of private life is even truer of public life. Romanticism opened the door to dangerously destructive passions, but utopias resulted in despotic bureaucracies.

Bureaucracy was the defining feature of the period. It was a very poor substitute for the holism of old, and its pedantic prescriptions were a naïve attempt to establish a framework for compulsory happiness. Utopias obviously cannot become a reality; as the word itself indicates, they are *u-topias* or 'non-places'. These utopias clearly could not satisfy individuals who were just discovering their personal freedom and who were especially eager to enjoy greater autonomy, particularly in the very private realm of love. In that sense, romanticism was less reactionary than it might seem. It is usually regarded as reactionary, whereas the utopians are usually seen as being on the side of progress. And yet the romantics did prefigure some very modern forms, whereas the utopians were caught in a trap of their own making because their holism was already archaic.

There were also other reasons why these utopias could never become a reality. The men who theorized these great systems, which were as moral as they were political, inevitably put too much of themselves into them without really realizing what they were doing – all the more so as they were dealing with the highly personal issue of love. A lot of individual desires were therefore institutionalized and turned into general theories. Those who simply tried to use these theories had their own fantasies and obviously did not recognize themselves in them. One man's most intimate thoughts cannot be applied to all men. Take the example of poor Auguste Comte and his utopia of the Virgin-Mother. The Virgin-Mother was in fact a direct product of his own history. As a young man, Comte had no interest in chastity, and actually married a prostitute (he later repudiated her). In 1845, he met a pretty young woman called Clotilde and fell madly in love with her. She had an interest in philosophy and admired Comte as a great thinker. They quickly become very close, but their relationship was based upon a misunderstanding. He dreamed only of taking her in his arms but Clotilde was not, to be quite blunt about it, physically attracted to him. She was sometimes bored by his long speeches about philosophy, which he saw as a form of flirtation. On 5 April 1946, Clotilde died at the age of thirty-one. Auguste never got over his unrequited desire for a beloved body that was snatched from his embraces by death. He had already had mental-health problems, and he now began to suffer a posthumous form of love-sickness. One of the first measures to be promulgated in his utopia was the 'duty to be an eternal widower'. It was sacrilegious for any man to remarry after the death of his beloved. This explains why a wife's death had, paradoxically, to be seen as a stroke of good luck: it freed the lover from her physical attractions and allowed him to attain a spiritual form of loving mysticism. Hence the idea of the Virgin-Mother. None of this theory would ever have seen the light of day if Clotilde had said 'yes'.

Whilst Auguste Comte turned his eyes to his secular heaven, other utopians had much more down-to-earth plans and were much more interested in matters carnal. Restif de la Bretonne, who belonged to the previous generation, came up with a plan for 'an island of joy' where no marriage could last for more than a year. He too had his secret obsessions (he was attracted to very young girls), and drew up plans for what he called a 'Parthenion'. This was, in his view, no frivolous brothel but a real public temple whose boarders were performing a civic duty. Being just as bureaucratically pedantic as Fourier, he defined its rules down to the last detail, choosing the flowers and perfumes, dividing everything into endless categories and even establishing a table of charges. Presumably, he could already imagine himself in his temple. He had little interest in women who were 'past it' (women who were still beautiful, but who were over thirty-six; the eighteenth century took an unforgiving view of such things), who charged between 6 and 12 *sous*. In his dreams, the 'sixth corridor' was his private realm; this is where girls 'aged between 14 and 16' waited for him (Restif de la Bretonne 1769: 126). But that is enough about Restif and his disturbing fantasies. Barthélemy-Prosper Enfantin is much more interesting. He was 'a handsome man of great stature, with a silky blond beard and the look of a man inspired . . . and was adored as though he was a Messiah' (de Planhol 1921: 224–5). He was well aware of how attractive he was, and he had no hesitations about theorizing his position. The high priest of his Church of Love (Enfantin himself) had to be a man whose radiant beauty and intelligence caused him to be 'loved in both the spiritual and the physical sense' and to be 'worshipped with ardent love' by his disciples (cited, de Planhol 1921: 228), and especially by his women-disciples. His aim was to liberate women by allowing them to enjoy the ultimate pleasures; God had commanded them to enjoy carnal pleasure. The polite society of the day, which was very prim and proper, took offence at this and put Enfantin on trial. He took advantage of this to address his disciples: 'When I tell the world what I am telling you here (and the time when I will do so is drawing nigh), we will be accused of preaching libertinage and orgies. The act that is for us the sign of the highest virtue will be described by them as debauchery' (cited de Planhol 1921: 230). Perhaps I am being a little harsh on Enfantin. He was the leader of a sect and he had his autocratic tendencies, but his project was, in its day, truly revolutionary as it was based upon the ideas of unfettered love, joy and physical pleasure. For the young people

who followed his example and rejected the bourgeois order,
Enfantin's utopianism was the dawning of a fabulous new age. A
new bout of fever was all it took to prove that love could once
again dominate the political stage.

BACK TO AMERICA

Enfantin established his community in an isolated house. Many
utopians dreamed, like Thomas More before them, of establishing
their alternative societies on islands. Others chose the wide, open
spaces of the New World. I therefore suggest that we go back to
the America that so disappointed Stendhal in the company of some
rather insane dreamers. America was the scene of many experimental attempts to base human relations on love, and some
hundred or so such communities were established in the young
United States. Many were very spiritually inclined, took a puritanical form of *agape* as a point of reference, and had a lasting
influence on the American mentality. The Shakers were an extreme
example. Originally from the Cathar lands of the south of France,
they spent some time living in exile in England before they succeeded in establishing their collective villages in the United States,
where they converted thousands of members to a Manichean faith
that preached radical abstinence. Other groups were much less
austere, and banked on a much more carnal and joyous vision of
love, either by espousing a secular and revolutionary utopianism,
or by concocting a subtle mixture of mysticism and sensual pleasure. The secular Etienne Cabet believed that both property and
wives should be held in common in the wonderful world of Icaria.
If a stranger coveted someone's wife, her husband ought to be
delighted: 'You would make both her and me very happy, and my
only desire is to make her happy' (Cabet 1845: 298). In 1848, a
group of Icarians set off to found a communist colony in Texas.
The encounter with the real world was harsh, and internal conflicts broke out; the adventure was over by the end of the century.
The American utopian John Humphrey Noyes was representative
of the religious strand. Originally a theologian, he had reached
the conclusion that the morality dictated by the Church could not
be divinely inspired because God spoke directly to each of us
(Noyes 1847). Everyone had to be liberated from the Church's

morality,[6] and especially from the constraints imposed by monog-
amous marriage. In 1879, Noyes came under suspicion of corrupt-
ing minors and fled to Canada. Even so, communities of self-styled
'perfects' flourished for more than thirty years all over the United
States.

All these groups distanced themselves from the great theoretical
constructs of the utopian thinkers. Pedantic details, categories and
classifications were of no practical relevance on adventurous expe-
ditions that went from one surprise to another. When they had to
improvise, they found that money was a much better means of
settling social problems than love. Everyone interpreted love in
their own way, and personal desires began to creep in. Paradoxically,
love had the opposite effect to that intended, and gave rise to
rivalries and personal clashes. And the only way to resolve such
conflicts was to give more power to leaders and to reinforce the
tyranny of organizations. Even with restricted groups that were
cut off from the rest of the world, love was not in itself enough
to define the rules of the game in any definitive way, no matter
whether it was seen as a universal value or a shared passion. And
so the utopias remained utopias and beautiful dreams. The few
that did not completely disappear (other than strictly religious
communities) survived only because they made a profit and went
over to a monetary economy. Jean-Baptiste Godin, for instance,
was one of the few to succeed in applying Fourier's theories (to
some extent). He created a 'familistery' (which was, for its time,
revolutionary) with a theatre, a school, a swimming pool and
comfortable housing built around his factory. His utopia was a
failure in human terms, but his brand of cast-iron stoves still sells.
John Humphrey Noyes established his community in Oneida in
New York State. One of his children went on managing the
group's business, rationalized it and began to concentrate on producing silverware. Outsourcing production to Asia made Oneida

---

[6] This was not a new idea. It goes back to the radical Manicheans and
is based upon the argument that whatever the body does is of no importance because it cannot damage the purity of the soul; the two worlds
are completely separate. The idea was picked up by Heroët, who became
Bishop of Digne. In his *La Parfaite Amie* (1542), he writes that, when
the soul is enraptured, bodies 'Can take their ease without thinking about
it / no matter when hands touch or mouths kiss'.

Limited a world leader (as they say) in top-of-the-range cutlery. Most of Enfantin's disciples were young engineers or graduates of the Ecole Polytechnique, and they soon found lucrative positions once they had recovered from their youthful excesses. Even the great guru himself became the administrator of a major railway company. Order had been restored – or almost restored. Enfantin never stopped dreaming. Like all utopians, he could not stop dreaming. He travelled the world and denounced the horrors of colonialism in Algeria. He almost became the man who came up with the idea for the Suez Canal. And he went in search of the 'Woman-Messiah' of the East in the belief that their sublime marriage would unite East and West . . .

Natural Harmony

We have often dreamed of a world ruled by love, but love proves, alas, to be a very difficult tool to handle. And so, the most grandiose projects ended in failure. And some, like romanticism, turned into their opposite: suffering turned into pleasure, darkness became light, and public failure turned into private success.

The history of love is a curious mixture. On the one hand, we have the long and fairly calm river of behavioural patterns that evolve slowly. That sometimes creates the impression that feelings and gestures change little and that the idea of love remained the same for centuries. On the other hand, we have the distant forges where categories of representations are manufactured, and they can change in quite spectacular fashion. Categories of representations are the prisms through which a given era sees the world, or collective ways of seeing and feeling things. Although our thoughts are very personal, we cannot think without these elementary instruments. We do not invent the languages we use; we use the words that are current within a given society. Similarly, we adopt, each in our own way, ready-made intellectual categories, and use them as points of reference in our day-to-day lives, as we can see from whole series of symbolic little marks whose origins have been forgotten. We have seen that there is a link between sex and darkness, and that it derives from Mani. I could just as easily tell you the very long history of the symbolism of hearts. There are always lots of hearts in amongst the flowers and chocolates on display in the shop windows on Valentine's Day, but they are in fact the product of very ancient and fantastic beliefs. Strange as it may seem at times, a detour to the forges where categories of representation are produced tells us much more about love than a systematic description of words and actions. It is true that the factory where new forms of loving are designed sometimes invent very little that is new, the dreamy utopians being only one example. But sometimes the opposite happens. What looked like a failure can have far-reaching effects, either directly or indirectly. Romanticism is the obvious example.

A host of intermediary processes come into play to make concrete individuals adopt representative categories. There is a great distance between the secret forges and everyday life, but thousands of little utopias that were either calmer or more discreet came into being midway between them. Unlike romanticism, they did not renounce this world and, unlike the dreams of the utopians, they did not take a revolutionary form. They had much more in common with the lived experience of love, and simply tried to enhance its benefits. And some of these pragmatic reformers also had considerable influence.

The belief in natural harmony was especially influential. The idea of natural harmony emerged just as Reason's grandiose projects were ending in failure, whilst Reason itself was laying the foundations for a cold and divisive society. According to sophisticated observers like Montaigne, the moral losses greatly outweighed the improbable gains that might be made. They argued that, on the contrary, an attempt should be made to re-establish a harmonious bond between human beings and the world around them, to rediscover some self-evident truths and to learn from those exotic civilizations that had managed to cultivate this wisdom. If that could be done, love would supply both the vital energy and the joys of life. Love was 'a waking, lively and cheerful agitation', and Montaigne happily recommended it to everyone and believed that there should be no limits to the search for 'sweet pleasures'. Nor should there be any limitations on sex, which was quite natural and 'the most noble, useful and pleasing' of all functions (Montaigne 2008 [1595]: vol. III, 237, 121). Montaigne was not the only one to think along these lines. He was representative of a general intellectual and artistic trend that challenged this new western civilization in the name of a mystical idealization

of nature. The trend found expression in a number of great
works, but also in works that reflected the spirit of the times
and that enjoyed considerable success in their day. 'The bucolic
myth spread throughout Europe during the baroque age, with
Montemayor's *Diane* in Spain, Sidney's *Arcadia* in England,
Honoré d'Urfé's *L'Astrée* in France, Guarini's *Le Berger fidèle* in
Italy, Optiz's *Pastorale de la nymphe Hercinie* in Germany . . . It
was a world-wide fashion' (Bologne 1998: 77). The myth centred
on the shepherd–lovers I mentioned earlier. These delightful por-
trayals of sylvan gallantry and gentle manners expressed a philosophy of life that was at once discreet and very ambitious. The
philosophy became more obvious as its proponents gradually
adopted an openly subversive stance. Its greatest representatives
were Jean-Jacques Rousseau and then the romantics, for whom a
fusion with nature was a central element in harmony. But theirs
was still a gloomy vision. They dreamed of a counter-world, and
of rejecting this world in the name of a dream and the emotions
it inspired. There was none of this in Montaigne. There was no
rebellion and no melancholy. The nature he evokes is not a distant
'elsewhere'; it is quite concrete, and it exists in the here and now.

For the 300-year period from the sixteenth to the nineteenth
century, the religion of nature permeated Europe deeply. It developed in stages and followed a number of fashions, celebrating,
first, shepherds, and then the 'noble savages' who glowed with
health and who were past masters of the arts of love. Travellers'
tales were a source of both enthusiasm and wonder. Monsieur de
Bougainville reported that, in his 'New Cithara' (known to its
natives as Tahiti), 'The prevailing climate is one of gentle joy and
every semblance of happiness' (Bougainville 1771: 198). He
described how they were welcomed by laughing men and naked
nymphs, and the loving rituals that followed on carpets of flowers
to the accompaniment of joyous music. 'Here, Venus is the goddess
of hospitality; her cult involves no mystery and every pleasure is
a feast for the nation.' European minds were understandably
astounded by such idyllic pictures. Nature was good and beautiful,
and it afforded all the virtues of harmony as well as intense
pleasure.

The god Plato called 'common love' has always tried to find the
fault lines that allow him to give his instincts a free rein. In puritanical societies, the god is provocative or subversive, and acts in

secret. When love's official persona is more attractive, he acts more openly. The religion of nature and its bucolic myths provided the backdrop for new expressions of physical desire. Whether or not they referred to these myths, libertines certainly persuaded the courts of princes to adopt more relaxed and more daring customs. Now that love was no longer associated with guilt or the Christian notion of the sinful flesh, it became a game.

Sadly, gentle nature proved incapable of resolving all problems. The extreme figure of the Marquis de Sade took it upon himself to rip up this idyllic picture. He too took the idea of nature as his starting point, but he reached very different conclusions: 'At no point does the nature that causes us to be born alone command us to treat our fellow men gently' (Sade 1797: 195). The nature that acts within us through the medium of our instincts urges us to free ourselves from all morality, to express all our desires and to act out all our fantasies: 'At all times, and in all places, all men must be there to serve your pleasures' (Sade 1797: 75). Those 'pleasures' may include cruelty, violence, torture or even murder: the pleasure of those who commit such acts is the only thing that matters! Even if a man commits homicide, 'it is nature that drives him' (Sade 2006 [1795]: 141). Sade shows no concern for his victims. The only thing that matters is the personal pleasure of someone who knows no boundaries. And where is love in all this? The Marquis's answer is very clear: 'Oh, lustful girls, give us your bodies as often as you can! Fuck, entertain – that's all that counts! But be sure to flee love!' (Sade 2006 [1795]: 95).

Having torn up the idyllic picture of a beautiful and benevolent nature, which he replaces with violent instincts, Sade denounces love in the name of selfish pleasure. Despite their unbearable inhumanity, Sade's writings still have an appeal that extends far beyond the narrow circle of perverse madness. One of today's great questions is whether or not our personal pleasure frees us from the obligation to think of others. Montaigne rightly described sexuality as something noble and pleasing, but our understanding of it is now so often perverted that it has come to mean simply exploiting one's partner. The liberation of the body has come to mean a selfish liberation, and this raises some very real problems: it no longer has anything to do with love, and everything about it militates against love.

4

Enter the Happy Couple

My story has taken us to some very strange places. It has taken us on a journey through politics and religion, which are far removed from personal feelings and one-to-one relationships. I have explained why: the mysteries of love lie hidden in the construction of the new intellectual categories which, hundreds of years after the event in some cases, still shape our conception of intimacy. We have seen a lot of failures, as love's somewhat insane dream of ruling the world never became a reality. In most cases, however, its public failures had an effect upon private life, made it more attractive and turned it into a world apart. It was a world that offered comfort and consolation to the unhappy individuals who had been assaulted and bled dry by a utilitarian society that was becoming increasingly competitive and calculating. And it was a world whose forms were in most cases the products of categories that had been elaborated elsewhere. 'Love was born of an idea of what love was' (Bozon 2005b: 592). Every kiss and every cuddle has to be related to this broader history. We would not kiss and cuddle in the way that we do if these religious and political battles had been different. Having looked at how the great categories were forged, we will now look at how they were used, manipulated and even distorted and at how they actually structured conjugal realities.

COPULATING WITHOUT SIN

Rome's Christians talked a lot about love, and their ideas were to turn the word upside-down. But when it comes to the way couples actually lived together in the real world, their contribution was, to say the least, problematic, and remained problematic for hundreds of years. The simple explanation is that they could not find a way out of the inextricable contradictions in which they found themselves. They could not agree about the question of marriage, let alone about the idea that relationships might, as the poet Terence had suggested, have something to do with emotions and pleasure – that was still in the distant future. They obviously wished to make it clear that they were not Manicheans, accepted that the species had to be reproduced, and therefore agreed to tolerate marriage, especially as the anarchic common-law marriages of the day did not offer a better solution. But where did marriage stand in relation to the purity that celibacy represented? This was, to put it mildly, a thorny question, as apologias for chaste solitude obviously gave rise to doubts about marriage. 'Copulation, the bodily humours, procreation, and consequently marriage – all were regarded with deeper repugnance than before' (Duby 1983 [1981]: 27). In St Jerome's view, marriage simply made fornication official, and was therefore accursed. Gregory the Great divided society into two: a celibate elite, who enjoyed direct communications with God, and inferior beings who married and who were therefore tainted. In an attempt to avoid damning the entire population, the more diplomatic St Augustine defined marriage as 'the least imperfect form of copulation' (Duby 1983 [1981]: 28). But even that definition left marriage at the bottom of the hierarchy of virtues: nothing could be higher than consecrated celibacy.

A lot of complicated intellectual work had to be done before marriage could be established as a sacrament, and as the dominant norm. A doctrinal distinction had to be made between marriage and the sins of the flesh. Sex within marriage was, it was therefore decided, moral. Whilst it was impossible to achieve the purity of Mary – a mother even though she was a virgin – the ideal was to imitate her as closely as possible by ensuring the biological reproduction of the species whilst avoiding the throes of sensual pleasure. Asceticism, or at least reserve, which were the symbolic values of celibacy, therefore became part of marriage. The doctrine was further perfected in the twelfth century and eventually became part of a coherent whole: marriage was ordained by God, it was a sacrament, and an expression of the love of God. Marrying therefore meant partaking of the love of God. Matrimonial love had more to do with spiritual mysticism than with physical contact. It wrought a minor miracle: physical union without sin. A degree of self-control was, however, still required and the emotions had to be repressed. Couples had to learn to make love without experiencing any great pleasure or passion.

None of this was easy. Rampant sexuality is not easily controlled, and a lot of people had to do penance. Although marriage gradually became the norm, new desires began to emerge at the end of the Middle Ages. The moralists began to mobilize, especially on the sexuality front. In the secrecy of the confessional, 'exaggerated physical' love, 'over-ardent' love and 'unnatural passions' began to suffer repression. The sexual act was for procreation and not pleasure. The sins committed by husband and wife were even worse than those committed outside marriage. A new front was then opened up as feelings began to suffer repression too. Until now, everything had seemed fairly simple. There was the love of God, which was unique, positive and transcendent and which bound the conjugal group together for life, and then there were coarse, pagan pleasures that had to be resisted. An intermediate position then began to be discreetly defined: it was 'a sort of profane love' that wanted to be accepted as 'true love' because it claimed to be 'honest' and 'modest' (Flandrin 1981: 53). Some theologians were up in arms about this sacrilegious suggestion that a man should prefer his wife to union with God, but their protests went unheeded. The long march that would lead to the modern idea of companionate marriage had begun.

LOVER OR HUSBAND?

When I say 'couple', I am referring to couples who married for life. Outside the institution of marriage, heightened passions had been making hearts beat faster ever since the days of courtly love and the Breton romances. Literature is a sort of laboratory for the future, and it experiments with new feelings. For the moment, they are no more than dreams; and when they can be expressed, they are expressed in the form of fiction. And yet the private fantasies that they inspire do begin to outline a possible future (Kaufmann 2008a). Literature – and not just great works of literature – therefore has to be taken seriously; more popular genres also invent the future, sometimes more so than great works. Where courtly poetry is concerned, let me recall some of its essential features. Despite the conventions of the day, the woman was the central figure, and she was worshipped by a suitor who put himself at her disposal. 'Wonderful', you might say. Unfortunately that dominant position was not without its disadvantages. While the knight was off performing great feats, the Lady simply had to stay at home and wait. He was developing a new art of seduction, and she simply had to react to his initiatives. Although it was the Lady who took the decisions, the way the roles were apportioned allowed the man to be much more innovatory and to develop forms of behaviour that remained a male preserve for centuries, and that are still a male preserve. Love was a form of conquest. In his study of the eighteenth century, Maurice Daumas comes up with a formula that well captures the great split between the two worlds: 'Before marriage, love is men's business; after marriage, it is women's business' (Daumas 2004: 36). It was up to the men to make the advances and to joust like valiant knights as the girls looked on. Because it fed on an impulsive male desire, their love was 'valiant, reckless and ready to fight' (Daumas 2004: 36). Once the man had made his conquest, his feelings vanished as quickly as they had appeared. Marriage was a different story: there were no conquests to be made inside marriage.

Women, on the other hand, were trapped into marriages that severely limited their horizons. Once conquered, they found it difficult to accept this sudden withdrawal, which was synonymous with emotional coldness. For women, introducing sentimentality into the relationship was a way of making their lives more intense and a way of taking the initiative. If men were the hero-seducers, women were the heroines who made marriage and what came after marriage an emotional business. In the late Middle Ages, women were still unable to make active use of sentimentality, but they dreamed of doing so – while they were reading novels, for instance. As access to legitimate literature was often forbidden to them, they used more popular literary forms to develop – sometimes in secret – the feminist tactic of using the emotions to improve their social position. At a slightly later date in Prussia, the Countess of Scheverin (who also read the great writers and the philosophers) explained how she and her cousin hid from their family to devour 'many a trifling and frivolous book' at night (cited Daumas 2004: 35). Although these novels, which were influenced by the courtly tradition, dealt mainly with pre-marital passions, it can be assumed that many of the women who read them also dreamed of more lasting feelings. Reading and discussing novels allowed women to quietly redefine their emotional expectations.

Those expectations gave rise to new suggestions, and those suggestions triggered a new and widespread interest in sentimentality. It began to develop at a very early stage with the astonishing writer known as Chrétien de Troyes. Chrétien was a true courtly poet who drew up detailed lists of the feats that had to be performed for the sake of the Lady. He also wrote for the Beautiful Lady known as Marie de Champagne. But as his choice of pseudonym indicates, he was a Christian too. He was a devout Christian who genuinely believed in the principles of marriage. Was it possible to reconcile courtly love with marriage? Chrétien accepted the challenge, and tried to achieve the impossible synthesis. And he succeeded in doing so in some of his stories, such as *Erec and Enide*, which was written in *circa* 1170 (now in Chrétien de Troyes 1991). The story in fact begins with a marriage, which is very surprising, given the courtly context. It was a love marriage. The couple were so happy together that Erec lost interest in tournaments and the other manly obligations that were incumbent upon knights. The courtly code had obviously been broken. Enide became aware of this, and began to play a very active role in the story. She shook her sleeping husband until he woke up so that he could win her heart anew by performing new feats. This wave of a magic wand appeared to re-establish the courtly code. The only difference was that all this happened within marriage, and that it strengthened the couple's marriage by sentimentalizing it. Chrétien de Troyes really was very clever.

It has to be remembered that courtly love was bequeathed us by the Cathars, and that one of their basic principles was to reject marriage in the name of the divine Light. I have explained how this gloomy, radical Manicheism was inverted to produce the colours and gallantries of courtly love. But it remained hostile to marriage. Chrétien de Troyes therefore brought about a new inversion, or a new stage within an inversion. He kept the feelings and perpetuated the idea that the Lady demanded constant attention and required her lover to outdo himself, but he made all this part of the institution of marriage (Markale 1987). Many other writers went on to follow his example, which goes to prove that this trend was part of a groundswell that affected the whole of Europe. In Spain, for instance, Garcia Rodriguez de Montalvo (whose tales of gallant knights were an inspiration to Cervantès) ends his *Amadis de Gaul* with a fine marriage (but only after many adventures, of course). In Masuccio Salernitanto's original story, which dates back to the fifteenth century, Romeo and Giulietta marry.

TWO LOVES IN ONE

'If a couple drink together, eat together and sleep together, that looks like marriage to me,' says a late medieval proverb (which also makes it clear that there was still no room for sentimentality within marriage), before adding 'But the Church has to sanction it' (cited Daumas 2004: 64). This was new: the Church obviously wanted to strengthen and control the institution of marriage by making couples adopt its rites and, above all, by imposing its morality. That was problematic for a number of reasons. Christianity is a loving religion, and it commands us to love our neighbours as ourselves. We must love all our neighbours, and *a fortiori* our closest neighbours. Simply eating, drinking and sleeping with one's husband was unimaginable. How could one do that without having any feelings for him, especially when the Church preached the need for universal love? It was unthinkable. If the Church was going to interfere with marriage, it therefore had to introduce a little love into that relationship. It did not really have to force itself to do so, given that the impetus behind the groundswell came from women. And that was the problem. If the floodgates were opened and if marriage became a matter of sentimentality, there was a danger that the whole psychic economy on which society was based would be thrown into turmoil. And women's expectations in this domain were worrying. Love partook of the divine essence. It was a grace that was bestowed upon married couples, and it demanded in return that they love God before all else. Husbands had to come second, and must not be allowed to interfere with that primary duty. That warded off the danger that things might get out of hand, or that human feelings would supplant the adoration of God, which might bring down the whole edifice.

How could anyone love her husband less than she loved God without offending God when everyone was dreaming of more intense inter-personal exchanges? The equation was obviously insoluble, but the heavy-handed repression of women's expectations might lead them to circumvent the institution of marriage, and might unleash anarchic passions. Sophisticated observers therefore pointed out that it was impossible to hold back the rising tide of a desire for more human feelings. Some even went as far as denouncing and criticizing extreme bigotry. How could anyone who claimed to be a Christian have so little love for her closest neighbour? She could not. In the eyes of God, her husband was her rightful lord, and he deserved better than this. One sixteenth-century author of handbooks on Christian etiquette finally lost his temper: what was the point of spending your time in churches and chapels if meals were not ready on time and if your poor husband was being neglected? 'The bed or the table where she serves her husband is the altar of God' (cited Daumas 2004: 216).

The idea of serving one's husband at table in the same way that one served God was not exactly revolutionary, to say the least. But in bed . . . The equation that the theologians and moralists could not solve centred on the marital bed. Copulation had long been tolerated because of the need for biological reproduction but it had been fenced in on all sides to avoid the danger of 'fornication', meaning pleasures, feelings and actions that were over-affectionate. A wife had to do her 'duty', but she must perform it as unemotionally and coldly as possible (husbands were more easily forgiven because their temperament was more 'sanguine') whilst thinking about something else (and ideally while saying her prayers to God). If she could not prevent herself from sinning by experiencing some lascivious emotions, she could then atone for her sins in the confessional. Hence the importance of quasi-magical rituals. Saying one's prayers at the foot of the bed, for instance, was a way of warding off the demons of pleasure. The need to do so become even more urgent (and unproductive) as relations between husband and wife became more emotionally based. But how could a woman honour her husband with the sustained, close attention that was demanded of her and at the same time remain cold and distant? New spaces where emotions could be expressed and exchanged were beginning to emerge, together with new forms of intercourse, such as conversation, letters, marks of consideration, and gallantry. But what was going on in bed?

The theologians and moralists came up with a solution by further refining the dialectic between the two forms of love. Given that God had made marriage a sacrament, loving one's partner was a way of loving God. There was no contradiction between the two forms of love, as they could be synthesized into a 'conjugal spirituality' (Walch 2002). This obviously implied absolute fidelity, but it also meant avoiding over-heated passion. The recommended behaviour now went far beyond mere reserve. Even pleasure was becoming acceptable . . . in suitable doses. Theologians like Tomas Sanchez in Spain and François de Sales in France were prepared to tolerate this containment of the instincts if it prevented adultery. François de Sales, who was on the point of being canonized and who could scarcely be described as a lecher, wrote in his eminently pious *Introduction à la vie dévote* ('Introduction to the Devout Life') that 'the simple pleasures of the sensual appetite', which extended beyond the strict need for reproduction, were 'acceptable' (cited Bologne 1988: 76). His book was a great success.

WOMEN USE TENDERNESS AS A WEAPON

The 'acceptable' pleasures allowed by the holy man were obviously open to many different interpretations, but the floodgates of the feelings and passions had been opened and they could never again be closed. And the way the two loves has been synthesized had already enflamed the imaginations of some men . . . and some women. In her letter to her husband, the princesse de Conti was inspired by her 'mad tenderness' to exclaim: 'As soon as we are together, our first thought must be to give ourselves to God completely' (cited Daumas 1996: 145). She may well have been thinking of God, but her first thought was to 'give herself'.

The conjugal landscape was undergoing far-reaching changes and women were on the offensive. Their main weapon was a culture of tenderness. Tenderness was by no means specific to women, and nor was it one of their biological attributes; it was a product of their historical position. At a time when they had no access to public life, tenderness was one of the few tools they could use to extend their influence by conquering a new conjugal domain that had yet to be imagined and constructed. And it was here that the novels that women read began to play a role by helping them to elaborate more sentimental relationships. The books men read had more to do with the conquest phase, and conveyed a more warlike image of love. Outside the spiritual domain, the word 'love' connoted recklessness and boldness. It was only in the seventeenth century, and especially the eighteenth century, that it came to be associated with tenderness (which had until then not been associated with love, and which tended, on the contrary, to suggest a state of weakness (Daumas 1996)) in the sense in which we now understand the term. All this reflected the influence of women. Before this upheaval took place, friendship (which was cultivated in exclusively male circles and networks) mattered more to men than love. By transforming the couple into a sentimental world, women could use it as a platform to draw men into what we can now recognize as a one-to-one relationship. The battle over sentiment was to have a huge influence on future developments. And men could put up no resistance; how can anyone resist tenderness?

This was a godsend for the theologians and moralists. Unlike the devilish depravities that could be dreamed up in bed, tenderness looked like an unthreatening feeling that was astonishingly close to Christianity's *agape* (Walch 2002). It implied paying a sort of gentle and loving attention to one's closest neighbour, and, one might add, charitable support, should it be required. At worst, it meant creating an affectionate environment (which was no crime). They failed to see that, virtuous as it may be, this feeling also implied something that was to have a decisive impact on the subsequent decline of religion: the principle of autonomy. Tenderness was not cultivated simply because it was a virtue; it was also something to be experienced for its own sake. The theologians should also have been intrigued by the fact that the philosophers of the Enlightenment were similarly enthusiastic about these tender conjugal feelings. It had proved difficult to make Reason the centre of society, but tenderness could help to make the virtue of benevolence part of the conjugal relationship.

INSTITUTIONALIZING HAPPINESS

For the moment, tenderness seemed to be a crystallization of the way the two forms of love had been synthesized into marriage. As mellow as the singing in church, marriage was a wonderful example of the divine-human hybridization that would, or so the dream would have it, produce a third kind of love. Because its gentleness evoked a certain moderation, it even suggested that lovemaking could be innocent of all passion. Marriage seemed to be an almost magical combination of all things: a solid institution and God's blessing, held together by the strange private *agape* that created a new ambiance characterized by thrills and the beginning of a search for happiness. This was only the very beginning of a process that would lead to what has become a veritable obsession with happiness. But the idea was already there *in nuce*: the purpose of marriage might be to make people happy and to allow them to enjoy being together. This meant paying attention to the other, and a loving tenderness.

After hundreds and hundreds of years of doubts and doctrinal conflicts, the Church had at last found the synthesis it had been looking for. It was all the more solid in that everything appeared to come from God, which made it feel like something eternal that existed outside real life. The same was true of the tenderness with which it manifested itself: it was the product of what François de Sales called 'a love that was completely holy, completely sanctified and completely divine.' 'Because it opened up the door to salvation, marriage became an equivalent to charitable works' (Daumas 2004: 106). Marriage was a generous act of self-sacrifice; one was completely at one's partner's service. Especially if 'one' was a woman. Now that the two forms of love had been synthesized, the seventeenth century saw a huge increase in the number of handbooks on etiquette that turned this new-style marriage into a veritable institution by codifying behaviour. These followed in the wake of the *Introduction à la vie dévote*, were usually written by priests and were essentially religious. Some were strict and severe, one example being Jean Girard de Villethierry's *La Vie des gens mariés ou les obligations de ceux qui s'engagent dans le mariage, prouvées par L'Ecriture, par les Saints Pères et par les conciles* of 1695 ('The Life of Married People, or the Obligations Incumbent upon Those Who Commit Themselves to Marriage, as Proven by Scripture, the Holy Fathers and the Councils'). Some laymen and clerics found the synthesis reassuring. Carried away by the new fashion for a sentimental tenderness, they wrote books that looked more like self-help manuals designed to guarantee not only the salvation of the soul but also happiness here on earth. The Révérend Père Thomas le Blanc, for instance, published a book with a title worthy of the self-help manuals that now promise us heaven and earth: *La Direction et Consolation des personnes mariées, ou les moyens infaillibles de faire un mariage heureux* ('For the Guidance and Consolation of Married People, or an Infallible Way to Make a Happy Marriage').[1] Claude Maillard, for his part, wrote *Le Bon Mariage ou le moyen d'être heureux* ('The Good Marriage, or How to be Happy'), but it has to be recalled that his perspective was still very spiritual (wives were asked to see themselves as reflections of a Church that had surrendered itself unto Christ (Carlin 2003)). In the view of an increasingly active minority current, these books still took too little account of human happiness. Catherine Lévesque, an educated woman who, as a widow, was free to speak her own mind, had no hesitation about denouncing the hypocrisy of the clergy. In her *Perfection de l'amour du prochain dans tous ses états par l'union de nos amours naturels aux amour de Dieu* ('Perfecting Love for One's Neighbour in All Its States by Uniting Our Natural Loves with the Love of God'), she openly asked the Church to stop shilly-shallying about 'those who perhaps marry because of some secret wish to be happy' (cited Walch 2002: 269).

The quest for happiness was not just an 'extra' that was more or less acceptable; it had to be central to married life, and it had

---

[1] The full title is even longer, as was often the case at this time. It ends with 'an abbreviated account of the lives of male and female saints who had many problems in their married lives'. The new alchemy of love was therefore not a simple process, as even saints could have many problems in their married lives.

to be something that was experienced for what it was. But because it now included the emotions, this fine synthesis was beginning, despite itself, to escape its strictly religious framework. By adopting the secular theme of happiness on earth that was so dear to the Enlightenment, these Catholic advocates of sentimentality were coming into contact with projects that had been elaborated outside the Church and were responding to the unspoken aspirations of society, and especially of women. They were to launch a whole trend – the search for happiness inside marriage – and we are its direct heirs.

Perhaps things were going too fast and too far. The rigorist wing, which was well represented by the Jansenists, foresaw that things would get out of control and launched a counter-offensive, arguing that there had to be a return to reserve and complete devotion to God. The emotional counter-offensive was not confined to continental Europe, and the U-turn was, if anything, even more sudden in England. The eighteenth century had seen the flourishing of a real celebration of companionate marriage, as was obvious from the immense popularity of Samuel Richardson's novel *Pamela or Virtue Rewarded*. In the second volume, the heroine exemplifies a new type of conjugal relationship that was both affectionate and tender. One hundred years later, Victorian society, in contrast, enforced a mood of strict prudery and a Puritanism which, as its very name indicates, drew upon the protestant ethic in order to intensify the repression. This chilly view of marital relations was not, however, a purely religious phenomenon, as a broad coalition of forces, many of them mobilized by men, also took the same view. Jean-Claude Guillebaud (1998) mentions both the medical profession (which was almost unanimous in its condemnation of pleasure) and the bourgeois spirit of the industrial revolution. The tendency to sentimentalize marriage came to a temporary halt. In France, three chapters of the *Introduction à la vie dévote* spoke quite favourably of the pleasures that could be enjoyed by married couples (subject, of course, to many restrictions); they were dropped from later editions (Walch 2002). A long period of wintry chill had set in: men and women were forced back into institutional (and hierarchical) roles, and there was no reason to worry too much about sentiment.

AMERICA AGAIN

It took almost a hundred years for this rigorist parenthesis to be closed in Europe. Things changed rather more quickly in the United States. The United States was a young country and it had not been affected by the First World War in the way that Europe had been affected. A curious phenomenon occurred there in the 1920s and, whilst it was not immediately obvious, it is of great relevance to our story. It was born of a combination of very different economic, social and cultural processes. In the late nineteenth century and at the beginning of the twentieth, a very active feminist movement had emerged in reaction to the prevailing Victorian morality (Illouz 2007). This movement was now led astray by seductive appeals that succeeded in recuperating its energy and its power to transform society. Industry had made spectacular progress, and could now supply appliances (such as electric irons and radios) that completely changed the domestic world. A new image quickly became dominant: the new woman was someone who could efficiently manage domestic modernity, and that image was given massive publicity by the newly important advertising industry. Specialists in marketing and communications spread the idea that women were at the forefront of progress in the home. There was a new mood of confidence about the way these changes were described, rather as though a whole new world was just waiting to be invented. It has to be said that this was not confined to the domestic economy. Now that the Victorian parenthesis was closed, a whole army of new professions (psychologists, social workers, marriage-guidance counsellors and so on) once more set about the task of institutionalizing happiness. Whilst many of these specialists were close to religious movements, the problematic had changed and was now dominated by science (Cott 1996 [1992]). Finding a hypothetical synthesis between two forms of love was no longer the issue; the one thing that mattered was a scientific analysis of conjugal relations that could make people happy, here and now. Attentiveness to partners and the need to communicate and show affection were now promoted with much greater energy and efficiency than in the eighteenth century, and women were in the forefront of this sexual revolution. As science did not share religion's inhibitions about sex, specialists cheerfully recommended new ways of finding and experiencing pleasure. The Kinsey Report (Kinsey 1953), for instance, demonstrated that the curve showing the incidence of 'petting' and orgasms rose steeply during this period. Relationships were once more being sentimentalized, but the process of change was now faster than ever (Cott 1996 [1992]: 79–80).

A number of very different factors contributed to this trend. Those that have already been mentioned (the hijacking of feminism, mass consumerism and the emergence of new professions steeped in the applied human sciences) combined with another factor that was, perhaps, even more important. I have already mentioned advertising, and the 1920s saw the rapid development of many media. Day-to-day life began to be invaded by sounds, images and stories. The cinema, to take only that example, attracted weekly audiences of between 100 and 115 million. What was the link between films and feelings? The themes, obviously. There were, of course, Westerns (for men), but love was the favourite theme. Some – *The Daring Years, Flaming Youth* and *The Queen of Sin* – were daring and thrilling, whilst others were more sentimental but they all had a happy ending (Cott 1996 [1992]: 80). 'Feminist defiance of the sexual division of labour was swept under the rug. Hollywood movies carried a celluloid image worth thousands of words, with the message that private intimacy equalled freedom and the push of an expensive automobile capped the search for the good life' (Cott 1996 [1992]: 90).

The old tradition of the romantic 'woman's novel' was taken up and greatly popularized by the film industry. 'It was then [during the early 1920s] that the happy ending had its heyday. Every plot had to lead up to a final lingering kiss against a background of roses or rich hangings' (Rougement 1983 [1940]: 234). Thousands of pictures of kisses were seen every day. Thousands of love stories were shown on-screen, and they set hearts beating and sustained the desire for a form of marriage that made more allowance for the emotions. But a note of caution is required here: passion has always been the enemy of legitimate love, and has always been a destructive force. Passion rebelled against the Church's attempts to put the love–domesticity synthesis on a moral basis, and it now resisted the efforts of American marriage-guidance counsellors to find a scientific explanation for what made a couple happy. The millions of women who adored Rudolph

Valentino in *The Sheikh* had probably only a very vague awareness of how ambivalent their feelings really were. They identified
with Diana, the heroine who rejects marriage in the name of
women's emancipation before falling madly in love with the handsome Arab prince and, after many an ordeal (and the revelation
that he is in fact of European origin), resolves to spend her life
with him. The happy (and morally acceptable) ending made it
possible to tone down both the original premise (the feminist
rejection of marriage) and the violent passion that takes Diana
into a different world. But within fifty years, the apparently harmonious conjugal love of 1920s America (a new synthesis that
reproduced the religious synthesis of the eighteenth century) would
be shattered into pieces.

MOTHERHOOD MUST COME FIRST

The situation in Europe was different, mainly because the First
World War had only a limited impact on Americans. You may
have a mental picture of women taking on new responsibilities as
they took the places of the men who had gone to the front. The
reality was rather different. Women replaced men to only a limited
extent, and were often confined to subaltern positions or to roles
that had female connotations, such as cleaning, keeping and
checking records, caring for the wounded, and feeding the home-
less. But at the imaginary level, the idea that men might lose their
dominant role generated a collective fear that had begun to be felt
with the first stirrings of the women's movement in the nineteenth
and the early twentieth century. This was a great period for
European feminism too. Françoise Thébaud (1994 [1992]) notes
that, paradoxically, the modest progress that had been made in
the world of work ushered in a conservative ice age in intellectual
terms. This probably had a lot to do with the fact that women
had adopted a new style and now displayed a bold confidence that
contrasted sharply with their old self-effacement: men were frightened of these strong, free women. It seemed that, after several
decades of progress in the direction of women's autonomy, the
process was speeding up, and that was too much. In the United
States, the energies of the women's movement were channelled
into a new conjugal domesticity; Europe (and especially the Latin

countries)[2] dreamed of a return to tradition where women were concerned.

The First World War may have looked like a good time for women, but plans were afoot for the restoration of order. The brave *poilu* was the emblematic figure who presided over the new cult of the dominant male: women had to be brought back into line. And they had to go back to being real mothers again. How could a good mother work outside the home? How could a good mother not devote herself completely to her children? In both Germany and England, the answer was obvious: a woman's place was in the home. In France, many women were now so integral to the production process that they could not be withdrawn en masse (Lagrave 1994 [1992]). That made the criticisms of women's autonomy even more virulent, especially as there was also a growing obsession with the falling birth rate. The real heroines were the mothers who had ten children and, from 1920 onwards, such mothers were awarded the Médaille de la famille ('Family Medal'). In Italy, Gina Lombroso's book *L'Anima della donna* ('Woman's Soul'), which reminded women that they had a mission to procreate, was a best-seller (De Giorgio 1992). In the meantime, America's marriage-guidance counsellors, in contrast, were advising women to have fewer children so that they would have more time to devote to their personal fulfilment within marriage.

For men whose identity had been undermined, this return to the old models felt like revenge. Many women were exhausted after all the efforts they had made, wanted a rest and were to some extent eager to return to domesticity, especially as the discourse of the moment was, as in the United States, popularizing the idea of a new, modern life. The Salon des arts ménagers ('Ideal Home Exhibition') showed the way to a revolution in everyday life. Unfortunately, the realities of domestic life were very slow to change. For most women, the revolution meant nothing more than a boiler for doing the laundry, tinned foods and electricity. The amount of time they devoted to housework actually increased, and conditions had scarcely improved. In 1948, only 4 per cent of

---

[2] The protestant ethic that had exacerbated the Victorian climate also encouraged the emancipation of women in northern Europe. John Milton's *Doctrine and Discipline of Divorce* (Milton 1643) is a good illustration of this paradox.

British households had a washing machine, and only 2 per cent had a refrigerator. In 1954, 42 per cent of French households still did not have running water (Sohn 1994 [1992]). Unlike their American sisters, European women had given up what they had in exchange for a future that was by no means certain. They had abandoned growing autonomy for the sake of a domestic modernity that failed to materialize. Life was dreary and women's horizons were very limited in the 1950s.

Dreams were all they had to fall back upon. European cinema may have been a long way behind Hollywood, but romantic novels tapped into the huge need for some escapism. The imaginary world they described was discreet, not to say secretive, but, even though they were mocked and forced onto the defensive, such novels paved the way for the great revolution that was to come. And this time, it did coincide with what was happening in America. Europe and America were out of step in the inter-war period, but that was simply because the contexts were not the same.

THE THORNY PROBLEM OF CHOOSING A PARTNER

Hollywood adaptations of romantic novels swamped and destabilized all attempts to institutionalize married bliss. In terms of the history of love, it is as though a real division of labour had been introduced. On the one hand, there were novels that inspired dreams. They were descended directly from the courtly love that had rejected marriage. The later versions were less influenced by Manicheism, but they still ended with a marriage and had nothing to say about what happened next. It was what happened before marriage that mattered: the meeting, the raptures of love, and the emotional construction of a new world for two. On the other hand, there were social and moral institutions like the Church, which gradually allowed marriage to evolve into a 'conjugal spirituality' that might lead to a quest for happiness. These institutions also valued sentimentality – a calm, tender sentimentality that always remained within the bounds of reason – but only after marriage. They still distrusted passion itself. Romantic novels, in contrast, were all about passion, even more so than romanticism itself. They caught the conjugal institutions' supporters completely unawares, especially in Europe, where the conservative reaction held out no prospects for women. And they caught them unawares because they were always very vague about this initial phase. They were convinced of the need to resist the passions. They were also convinced that marriages could not be based upon sentiment alone. They were not, on the other hand, sure of what they should replace it with.

And yet the original idea had seemed brilliant. Reason was divinely inspired, and Love was a grace that came down from heaven. The individual who 'freely' 'chose' his or her wife or husband was therefore guided by divine Reason and divine Love, which told him or her who his or her (life) partner would be and determined how his or her feelings for that partner should be expressed. It was in fact God who did the choosing. As for the feelings involved, they were quasi-divine and therefore had to last for ever; there was no room for any doubts. This fine intellectual synthesis allowed (at least in theory) the Church to take a revolutionary stance towards the private emancipation of the individuals concerned. The idea of freedom of choice was, that is, a direct assault on the traditional and conservative power of families. A number of cases were recorded in which priests protected young lovers from the will of their parents, most of them in Spain (Casey 1985). But, as a general rule, 'freedom of choice' was a topic for bitter discussions, and 'choice' was restricted to a narrow circle of suitable marriage candidates. It gradually become obvious that the Church's fine synthesis would not last for very long: human love was not the love of God, and love and Reason were forces that pulled individuals in different directions. Families tended to be in favour of Reason, and put forward lots of arguments to try to convince the reluctant lovers that they were right. The young couple longed to experience the emotional thrills described in the novels they had read. In the view of their families and the local priest, such feelings had nothing to do with the new and private *agape* that was inspired by the grace of God. Hence the endless debates about the young people's 'inclinations', to use a contemporary term that means precisely what it says. It was perfectly legitimate to be quietly 'attracted' to someone ('We are talking about love, damn it!'), but passion or heightened sensuality could not be tolerated. Some 'seducers' were even sentenced to death. Couples had to be kept under close supervision, and detailed definitions of 'acceptable' feelings had to be supplied. Every detail was therefore analysed. Even beauty was analysed. Most sixteenth-century treatises took the view that beauty was not to be trusted, and that no one should marry 'with their eyes'. But in the seventeenth century, the attractions of the body began to become more obvious, and the moralists had no choice but to accept the importance of beauty. They therefore tried to define a less problematic role for it. 'In the new economy of salvation, beauty became a reflection of grace' (Daumas 2004: 131). It was a gift from God. '(Divine) grace, (physical) beauty and (conjugal) tenderness formed a triad of triumphant values' (Daumas 2004: 131).

All these efforts were in vain. The irresistible rise of sentimentality, which was sustained by the reading of novels, frustrated all attempts to control it, and escaped all the moralists' subtle definitions. The eighteenth century saw more and more quarrels between lovers and their families. And the rise of romanticism led to a sudden rise in the number of quarrels.

OF THE IMPORTANCE OF CHEAP SERIALS

I have already talked about the destructive passions inspired by romanticism, and about its political failures. I have also described how it was criticized by theologians, doctors and the bourgeoisie at a time when attempts were being made to restore a puritanical sense of order. During the second half of the nineteenth century, romanticism was put on trial 'on all grounds and in all countries' (Bologne 1998: 143). I have also described how Flaubert, who had played at being a romantic when he was passionately involved with Louise, declared that he was 'tired of grand passions, exalted loves, sentimental love affairs and howling despair'. He was typical of the literary avant-garde as a whole, which now began to distance itself from romanticism in the name of realism: writers wanted to stare both society and the emotions full in the face. As they distanced themselves from romanticism, their criticisms became barbed and were even tinged with contempt. Having been converted from the black to the pink, the early radical romanticism that had once produced such powerful works now began to indulge in 'a gradual profanation of the myth, its conversion into rhetoric'. The myth opened 'on to a crowded main road, such as people stroll along on Sundays to watch the big fine cars go by and to complain of the speeding' (Rougemont 1983 [1940]: 240, 232). The mystical passion of old was diluted by the stereotypical romantic adventures described in what we would now call 'airport novels', and this degenerate romanticism sickened those who sneered at it in the fashionable salons. Real literature could not compromise itself with this vulgarity.

I am talking about the social implication of these works rather than their literary qualities. And the historical irony is that this 'trashy literature' proved to be of some considerable importance. It paved the way for the cultural revolution that we know so well, and for its attempts to define a new role for passion. Literary masterpieces, in contrast, were getting nowhere, despite their glittering style. The smart salons had failed to notice what was brewing in the lower depths. 'Masterpieces revealed less to us about the descent of the myth into manners than mass-produced novels, popular stage successes, and, above all, films. The real tragic element in our period has been diffused in mediocrity. Therefore to be truly serious implies an understanding, and the rejection or acceptance, of what moves or stirs the masses . . . with a force that the mind still finds it repugnant to gauge' (Rougemont 1983 [1940]: 232–3). Denis de Rougemont then demonstrates that the stereotypical content of these plays and novels simply reproduces, in a highly codified form,[3] the principles of courtly love. The 'eternal triangle' of *théâtre de boulevard* reduces the myth to 'proportions suitable for modern society. King Mark is become the Cuckold; Tristan, the junior lead or gigolo; and Iseult, the idle, dissatisfied wife who reads novels' (Rougemont 1983 [1940]: 233–4).

So it is time to talk about the women who read these novels. One of the reasons why the smart salons were so contemptuous of this trash is that romantic novels were read mainly by women.

THE ENDLESS PATIENCE OF WOMEN

Women were excluded from politics, economics, theology and science, and for hundreds of years the emotions were the only

---

[3] For a description of how this coding functions in the modern romantic novel, see Péquignot (1991).

things that allowed them to add spice to their lives and to make their presence felt in society. In order to do so, they had to be cunning and to appropriate things that were not meant for them. Novels of chivalry, for instance, were intended for a male audience, and were full of warlike exploits. But women also read them avidly, often in secret. In her story of her life, St Teresa, for example, describes how (before her conversion) she would hide away and, without her father's knowledge, plunge into her books: 'I was so enthralled by it that I do not believe I was ever happy if I had not a new book' (Teresa of Avila 1957 [1565]: 26). As we know, her passion subsequently inspired her to develop more spiritual interests. Most women did not share that destiny, but they did share Teresa's interest in the (human) passions. They did not read the same books as men, who were more interested in reading about glorious feats of arms. And that had an influence on the development of literature and encouraged the rise of the romantic novel, with all its tumultuous passions. And this in turn had an impact upon how novels in general were viewed. When he was persuaded, despite his better intentions, to write novels, Jean-Jacques Rousseau warned his readers in the preface to his *La nouvelle Héloïse* (1761), that this was probably a book for women. He was being ironic, but the irony could not mask his disquiet. This was, he claimed, a book for women who liked to indulge in daring daydreams . . . but who remained virtuous, of course. Novels in general were not recommended reading for girls: 'No chaste girl has ever read a novel.' And besides, any girl who dared to read *La nouvelle Héloïse* was 'done for'.

I have been talking about women who read novels, but we must not forget the women who wrote them. For a long time, women were barred from writing, just as they were barred from any involvement in politics or science. Once more, they had to be cunning. Madame de Lafayette published *La Princesse de Clèves* anonymously. Closer to home, George Sand had to dress up as a man, and Colette had to write under her husband's name. The earliest women writers were violently criticized and mocked by men. Molière turned them to ridicule. The main complaint was easily formulated: women writers were mawkishly sentimental, and could not cure themselves of their habit of writing about things that were of no interest. And to make matters worse, their style was pathetically bad. But it was because the emotions had for so long been the only weapon that women could lay their hands on that they placed so much emphasis on them. As it became clear that they were not talking about things that were of no importance, this proved to have far-reaching implications. The male-chauvinist and elitist contempt in which they were held was in stark contrast with their actual achievements, as women-novelists were in synergy with a very broad readership that even included working-class women. Romantic women novelists (and a few men) used sentimentality to transform society. Although they were not fully aware of the revolutionary implications of what they were doing, that is what gave them the energy to write.

And they needed all the energy they could summon, as the critics were becoming even more contemptuous. The more writers created simplified forms to meet the expectations of their popular readership (and before long they would be illustrating their stories), the more the smart salons laughed at them. And as it became obvious that most of these readers were women, the comments became outrageously sexist. Annik Houel (1997: 56) cites the revealing comment made in a journal dating from 1913: 'Serialized novels do as much, if not more, damage to the brains of women as alcohol does to the brains of men.'

PASSION TOPS THE BILL

The fashion for serial novels, which derived from the tradition of romanticism, became more and popular, but the novels themselves were published discreetly and were often read in secret. Serial novels began to appear towards the end of the nineteenth century, when they were published in instalments in newspapers. They became increasingly sentimental and were read mainly by women, who adopted the habit of cutting them out and binding them into book form (Houel 1997). The years leading up to the First World War saw the appearance of the *romans roses* series. These novels were written 'for families and girls', were intended to 'improve their moral education',[4] and therefore made sure that the passions

---

[4] Advertisement for the 'Romans Delly' series, which ran to over 100 novels – cited Péquignot 1991: 70).

were channelled in acceptable directions. During the inter-war period, the stories published as supplements to the new women's magazines added to what was already an abundant out-put. The air was full of love songs broadcast on the radio and played on gramophones, and they gave rise to a new kind of excitement. In terms of romantic films, Europe obviously did not have the same power as Hollywood, but it made a spectacular effort to catch up in the post-war years. Specific media such as photo-novels also helped to popularize this trend (Henry 1993). This very specific genre, which is symptomatic of the size of the female audience for romance fiction, emerged suddenly and on a huge scale. It first emerged in Italy, with titles such as *Grand Hotel* and *Bolero*. It was spectacularly popular, and its first stars – who included Gina Lollobrigida and Sophia Loren – soon became film stars too. In France, Cino des Duca began to publish *Nous Deux* magazine in 1947. *Nous Deux* obviously avoided any mention of actual sex, but a scornful Roland Barthes described it as 'more obscene than Sade'. Christian organizations worried about these apologias for passion. But none of these anathemas could hold back the rising tide, and the number of titles steadily increased. Before long, *Nous Deux* was selling over 1 million copies every week.

The 1950s saw the apotheosis of romance, which established an even closer link between women and love. Romance was initially a 'secret' literature of consolation but, although it has always been disparaged by everyone, it is now a very public phe-nomenon. Denis de Rougemont spent some time in the United States during this period, and was especially struck by cinema's power (Rougemont 1983 [1940]: 16–17). In his view, the myth of passion had been degraded to the level of mere romance. Stendhal would have been surprised by this very different (and female) side to America. Women were taking their revenge. They had long been denigrated and humiliated, but they had also been very patient (and sometimes vaguely ashamed) and had succeeded in putting passion on public display. It could now rival the very male figure of the calculating individual and openly put itself forward as a model. Except that . . . Except that the economy was booming, and had unleashed a lot of spending power and the emotions that went with it. Except that the repetitive codes of romance were far removed from real life and were the stuff of dreams rather than guides that taught us how to behave. And except that nothing had changed: the man was still the dominant partner in any relationship.

The feminists had not been fooled. They joined in with the chorus of men and intellectual know-it-alls, and criticized senti-mental romances just as harshly.[5] Passion was a trap, and it inevi-tably led to greater submission on the part of women. Even more critical of poor women readers than the men, they failed to make any distinction between the revolutionary potential of romance fiction and the alienated forms it adopted in the present climate, which could indeed subordinate women still further. The least that can be said is that they failed to reorient romance along more liberating lines, even though it would have been perfectly possible to do so. Leaving passion to one side, Maurice Daumas (2004) shows that, for several hundreds of years, one of the contradic-tions that plagued love was the contradiction between its liberat-ing and egalitarian potential – freedom of choice, reciprocal emotions, autonomy from institutional injunctions – and the mor-alists' attempts to force it into the mould of continued male domi-nation. Making clever use of the writings of St Paul ('Husbands, love your wives, even as Christ also loved the Church'; 'Wives submit yourselves unto your own husbands, as unto the Lord' (Ephesians V: 25, 23)), the moralists established a subtle distinc-tion between a male love that remained abstract, if not distant, and a female love that was very concrete and that implied an absolute self-sacrifice. It was this definition, and only this defini-tion (which allowed male domination to be reproduced) that made women subordinate. Love itself did not do so. And nor did passion, whose courtly origins demonstrate how it could once work to women's advantage. Perhaps a historic opportunity was missed here.

It might be argued that a missed historic opportunity was nothing compared with the immense task of liberating women. And that was a task for women themselves. Their liberation could not come about soon enough. Wasn't all this confused talk of passions a distraction from the fight for equality and auton-omy? After hundreds of years of inequality, the need for women's

---

[5] Bruno Péquignot points to the violence of their criticisms and analyses their assumptions by taking Michelle Coquillat's *Romans d'amour* (Paris: Odile Jacob, 1988) as an example.

liberation was so urgent that anything that helped to keep them in a subordinate position had to be criticized, and no one had time to go into all the details. But even if the need had not been so urgent, this mass interest in sentimentality did, despite its mawkishness and its stereotypical codes, contain the seeds of an alternative vision of an individual who had not been reduced to being just a calculating egotist. But for that vision to develop, the movement would have to have ceased to be an exclusively women's movement, women would have had to free themselves from the sentimental codes that made them subordinate to men (Radway 1984), and something inspired by radical romanticism would have had to give the movement a much greater impetus.

Romance was criticized on all sides and it retreated into its ghetto. Forced onto the defensive, it clung to archaic points of reference rather than inventing new ones. And it in fact had very little impact on the real world and was confined to the realm of consoling dreams. Jean-Louis Flandrin (1981) notes that it was actually in the last quarter of the nineteenth century that the idea of marrying for love really took hold. Even in 1959, one survey revealed that only one couple in five claimed to be marrying purely for love (Houel 1997). Despite 300 years of romantic novels, despite the 'inclinations' that were tolerated by the moralists, and the cult of romance, in real life the choice of a partner was emotionally poor and bound by social conventions. The novel does have the power to invent the future – but not automatically, and not in the immediate future. 'The discourse of love is slowly distilled in day to day life' (Martuccelli 2006: 204). Sometimes it is distilled very slowly indeed: it is difficult to use dreams to change the real world, and it is easy to become discouraged. But it would be a mistake to conclude that daydreams about love are nothing more than illusions. We do, however, have to take stock of the distance that for so long divorced what went on in the imaginary world of romance from what happened in the real world.

The life of Gabrielle is proof of that. I interviewed Gabrielle when I was researching my *Premier Matin* (Kaufmann 2002). Her story exemplifies, I think, the realities of life before the emotional upheavals of the 1960s. I cannot resist the temptation to tell her story as it is very instructive in that it exemplifies an important moment of historical transition from one world to another.

GABRIELLE: BETWEEN TWO WORLDS

Gabrielle had begun to 'go around with' André in secret. And then she told her parents. Her mother had her doubts, but her father seemed to be more understanding even though he did not make that entirely clear. 'No one said anything in so many words, and we did not go into all the details. But we sensed that we had my father's consent.' Things took a turn for the worse when André's family learned that Gabrielle's parents did not go to mass and that (worse still) their future daughter-in-law had gone to live in Paris (for work reasons). They asked their priest to look into the matter, and Gabrielle had to face some embarrassing interviews. 'They were afraid that I might not be respectable enough. The priest even asked us to stop seeing each other for a while to see if we really did mean a lot to each other. I took that very badly' – especially as this was happening in 1968, and the world around them was changing very fast. The priest's harangues seemed to belong to a different time. Gabrielle and André more or less 'went underground' so that they could go on seeing each other. 'We couldn't have done that five years earlier.'

Was Gabrielle in love? The way she tells her story suggests that her initial feelings reflected her struggle against social adversity, and that they developed into something else when they went public with the news that they were an item. 'When it all started, I did ask myself if he really was the One. Of course I did.' Then there was the complicity of 'going underground'. For two years, they secretly had breakfast together (they met in the morning, and did not spend their nights together!). When their decision to get married was accepted by their parents, she was able to express her emotions more openly. 'I was in love, I was going to be married, and nothing could stop that . . . nothing else existed!' She was in love, deeply in love. The striking thing about her story is that the institutional side of marriage seemed to be more important than anything else. It was the idea of marriage that really excited her, rather than her personal feelings for André. I asked her to talk about her 'first morning' with André, and it is highly significant that she chose to talk about the morning after their wedding night. A fortnight before that, the couple had spent their first 'night of love' together, in greater secrecy than ever.

In their own way, they were rebels and, in keeping with the spirit of the times, they refused to follow the conventions. They probably did desire one another, but it would be an exaggeration to say that they were part of the sexual revolution. And besides, Gabrielle could remember almost nothing about that night. 'It didn't really make any impression on me.' Their wedding night was a very different matter. That was an emotional awakening. And she remembers it very clearly.

They did not have a good night. André had forgotten to bring his pyjamas. Being very shy, he did not feel at ease with Gabrielle. The worst thing was that he was panic-stricken at the idea of the ritual that would inevitably take place next morning. 'He knew very well that everyone would come to get us out of bed.' That almost put him in a bad mood because he had forgotten his pyjamas. He spent the night worrying about his pyjamas, slept very badly and found it difficult to perform as expected. 'We almost messed that up.' When all the gang turned up in the morning, he barricaded the door. The assault team found a ladder. 'Fifteen or so of them piled in, and the situation got out of hand.' André refused to get out of bed. So the visitors perched on the other side of the bed to take the ritual photo. The bed collapsed in a crash of splintering wood. Anyone would remember a morning like that. But appearances can be deceptive: the story may well be funny (for everyone but André), but it is also testimony to the lasting influence of collective rituals. Now that she had got over the excitement of their secret meetings, Gabrielle was quite happy to conform to tradition. The breakfasts and their one night of love had been the only signs of a modernist desire for greater personal autonomy. When she got married, however, the strength of tradition and the power of institutions proved to be too great. 'That was that. I was getting married. And when I did the deed, it was with him. It could have been someone else, but it was him. That first morning was the beginning of our future together, and in some ways the future had already begun.' And now all they had to do was to go with the flow.

And yet Gabrielle did realize that the world was changing around her. 'If you slept with a boy, it was with the boy who was going to be your husband. I used to know girls of my age who slept with boys, and it was just a one-night stand. That was beginning to happen too.' The only thing that is wrong with Gabrielle's story is that the dates are not quite right. It is very typical of what was happening at the beginning of the 1960s, and not at the end of the decade. Even before the political explosion of '68, a lot of things had begun to change. Society was dancing to a different beat. Young people were becoming bold enough to demand a new autonomy, no matter what their parents thought. Dress codes were becoming much less formal. Bodies (and especially women's bodies[6]) were no longer subject to the old rules and were being liberated as the Pill overcame the fear of pregnancy. And to complete the defeat of the disciplines of old, sexuality suddenly became an autonomous realm. The body had taken on a new importance and individuals were in charge of their own destinies. The new autonomy of sexuality was closely associated with the emancipation of women, and this meant that nothing would ever be the same again. Romantic novels had tried for centuries to demolish the institutional fortresses and had failed. Within the space of just a few years, the fortresses crumbled as sexuality was liberated. There was just one small problem: the emotions.

THE AMBIGUITIES OF SEX

The life-style revolution of the 1960s would probably not have had the same impact without the energy of sexual liberation. Gabrielle's story shows how terribly constrained private life could be, even in a society where individuals were already beginning to discover a new autonomy. Something had to give, and it did give. The explosion could, however, have taken a different form, especially where the crucial issue of the sex/feelings articulation was concerned – particularly as the desire for liberation that was trying to find ways to express itself also affected the emotions, albeit in more discreet terms. This sentimentality made no secret of its political ambitions. The beat generation that emerged in the wake

---

[6] It was in 1964 that women began to sunbathe 'topless' on French beaches. That is highly significant. Women who had lingered shyly in the shadows, wearing headscarves and with their eyes lowered, had suddenly moved centre-stage and were enjoying a new freedom that intimidated men who, from this point onwards, began to lose their dominant position within private relationships.

of Jack Kerouac, and then the 'Peace and Love' movement were probably the last utopias to be based upon love. In Jean-Claude Bologne's view, there was 'a definite romantic component to this anti-materialism' (Bologne 1998: 193); more importantly, there was also a considerable element of spirituality in this quest for a purified love that could change the world. As in the nineteenth century, this utopianism took the form of experiments in living in small-scale communes (the difference being that the new model was neither bureaucratic nor pedantic). The experiments were short-lived and ended in failure, mainly because, whilst it was assumed that sex was all-important, it was divorced from feeling. Virginie Linhart, who was a child at the time, recalls that: 'Politics suddenly disappeared from our everyday world. Its place was taken by sex. We'd been living in a world in which everything was political, and now everything was sexual' (Linhart 2008: 140). The paradox is that the new emphasis on sex led to pitiless competition in a world where everyone dreamed of harmony. Jealousy was denounced as a bourgeois value.

> What struck me is that it was like living in a community of apes. There was one dominant male. All the women were in love with him and he slept with all of them, and the other males were conned. Doing away with power relations was one of the favourite themes of the times. But I think power relations became even worse. (Claudia Senik, cited Linhart 2008: 143)

Although it had a great influence on general issues, such as the rejection of war, the romantic current that associated sex with feelings was in fact a minority current, especially when it came to the way individuals behaved in their private lives. Love was subordinated to sexual liberation, which became a goal in itself and which was not subordinated to feelings. Love was no longer something that bound people together: it was just a source of pleasure. Another historic opportunity had probably been missed.

There was nothing new about this tendency to see sexuality as something autonomous, and it too was the product of a long history. Remember the new literary avant-garde's criticisms of romanticism and its haughty disdain for romantic novels. More sophisticated analysts began to have their doubts about love itself. According to Marcel Proust, being completely in love inevitably meant possessing the other, sucking the lifeblood out of her, and experiencing the 'horrors of love' (Grimaldi 2008). Desire had to be handled with great subtlety and kept at a distance. Others denounced sentimentality in even harsher terms. Alberto Moravia concluded that love 'was a ridiculous, naïf sentiment' (Bologne 1998: 176). As for Charles Bukowski . . . well, I'd rather not talk about Charles Bukowski. For similar reasons, I would rather not talk about the current fashion for a women's literature that uses sexuality as a weapon against sentimentality in a deliberately provocative way (Bozon 2005a). Staring reality in the face, or singing the praises of sex for the sake of sex, became the ultimate sign of an uncompromising modernity and freedom. Feelings did not get a good press, and they still do not get a good press.

As a result of the discovery of nature in the eighteenth and nineteenth centuries, and of the emergence of the great materialist philosophies, feelings, and especially loving feelings, came to be seen as nothing more than illusions. Schopenhauer thought that love was a mug's game. Freud's ideas caused a revolution by showing the extent to which sexuality influences us without our realizing it and structures our personalities during childhood, but he regarded love as a form of alienation, and passion as a form of infantile repression that bordered on psychosis (Alberoni 1994). Jean-Claude Bologne points out that, according to the father of psychoanalysis, the emotion is no more than 'egotism, a projection of fantasies, and a mirror-reflection of our own drives. You do not love a woman; you love an ideal image which has nothing to do with the woman you say you love; it has to do with your mother' (Bologne 1998: 170). The political thinkers who came after Freud and who used sexuality as an instrument of social liberation were all cast in the same ideological mould. Wilhelm Reich (1951 [1936]), that apostle of sexual liberation, called upon us to cast off all our chains, including our emotional chains. Herbert Marcuse (1955) chose to say nothing about the emotions, and Anthony Giddens (1992) notes with some surprise that Marcus contrives to say absolutely nothing about love in his studies of the relationship between sex and society.

The world in which we live is a product of all these developments, and it is so fragmented that we find it difficult to pick our way through it. Sexuality is highly ambiguous, and its attempts to give a meaning to life are constantly frustrated. At times, it takes the form of a pleasant technique for achieving well-being. At others, it speaks the language of competitive sport (Luhmann 1990 [1982]). At times, it dreams up a 'concrete utopia' that has less and less to do with a strict heterosexual monogamy (Chaumier 2004: 146), and other times it leads us into depressing blind alleys. And love has become more elusive than ever. 'Of course love still exists – but for whom, in what form and for what purpose? How can we grasp its meaning when we are not sure what we can do with it? How can we appropriate a good that is still vital if we no longer know how to take hold of it?' (Heinich 2003: 94).

I will break off my story here. We now have to look at love today. We have to look at its complex foundations, analyse its subtle components and look at the contemporary issues that are involved. But, as we shall see, these contemporary issues have something to do with my story, especially as the war between the two rival forms of love that we have identified is still raging, even though they both want to bring us happiness.

5

In Search of Happiness

The Economic Error

I share your indignation, my dear Isolde. You are quite right. The world is topsy-turvy, and in a way we have all fallen for an intellectual con trick. I have explained how society came to be centred on a certain model of the individual, and how that model then became the ultimate principle that regulates the world. (Partly because love, being unstable, contradictory and elusive, proved not to be a serious candidate for the role.) Business is now trying to impose its management principles in every domain (Gaulejac 2005; Marzano 2008). And an economics decked out in mathematical equations has become the socially dominant science. Now, economics is based upon the idea that human beings are cold, calculating animals. And that is the source of all our problems. It leads to a world of intolerable injustices in which one semi-literate, arrogant trader is worth a thousand times more than a dedicated youth worker. And it now quite simply raises the question of how the system is to be reproduced. It used to be based upon trust, but the crisis has destroyed that trust and people are beginning to have their doubts.

Economic models are in fact no more real than the dreamiest expressions of romantic passion. They contain a grain of truth, but only a grain. Calculating individuals do exist, but they have not always existed and there have never been many of them – which is just as well! Mathematical models are, like romantic passion, ideal schemata that are always just out of reach. They simply represent trends, and trends have a structural effect only when everyone shares the same belief. And the whole problem is that no one trusts the models these days. The economists tell us that we have to re-establish trust because everything is based upon trust. Upon trust! Or in other words, upon a feeling – one of the finest feelings in the world. The financial world is beginning to discover that it functions on the basis of a feeling! Then how can it go on believing in the chimera of a cold, emotionless individual? No, my economist friends, you have to rediscover – we all have to rediscover – the real world of human complexity, and the untold treasures that lie hidden in the multiple recesses of the human personality. We have to open up the black box that contains our emotions and our dreams. Human beings are not cold, calculating animals. And they are all the better for it.

The crisis is so serious that even the financial experts are beginning to talk about the need to 'regulate' capitalism. The word 'regulate' has suddenly become very fashionable. The general idea is to correct the most blatant excesses, such as the bonuses that no one can really understand because there are so many zeros, and exotic tax havens for impenitent tax-avoiders. But the problem is much, much bigger than that. The crisis is forcing us to ask questions about the meaning of these incredible inequalities, about our civilization's scale of values, and about the 'materialist sickness' (André 2009: 296) of the commodified world that is, we are told, all there is to life. And we have to ask questions about the root of all these evils: the unfounded assumption that the strange model of a selfish, calculating individual is a valid model (all the hard work that went into promoting it was quickly forgotten about). Does anyone really believe that we can build a flourishing civilization on the basis of calculating selfishness? There is a growing awareness that we obviously cannot.

THE NEED FOR LOVE

This harsh, unforgiving world of competition and calculation is generating a huge demand for love. There has probably never been a greater need for affection and comfort in any society.

Unfortunately, there is now a contradiction between the couple – normally seen as the source of love and solace – and the autonomous individual of advanced modernity. In yesterday's society, a partner was a partner for life, come what may, and till death us do part; a partner now proves to be an associate who can be dismissed at a moment's notice, and someone we quietly evaluate out of the corner of our eye. Even when they are in love, autonomous individuals cannot stop themselves from testing out their partners, and will decide to break off the relationship if it does not live up to expectations and does not make them happy. Not being happy is intolerable, and there is now a slogan: better to live on your own than with a partner you do not like. In Europe, one person in three now lives alone, and that proportion continues to rise steadily as the trend for individual emancipation moves from the countries of the north to the south (from Scandinavia to the Mediterranean) and spreads from the big cities into the countryside. But is it possible to be happy without other people? Of course not. His majesty the individual may well lay down the law, but the long laments about the lack of love are growing louder. All would be well if passion could sweep us off our feet, just as it does in romance fiction. But that is not what is happening: we always have our doubts and we are always in two minds. On the one hand, we want love, commitment and altruistic self-sacrifice; on the other, we look at things objectively, and we need some space to ourselves. Relationships are now based upon a contradictory dream: we dream of being with someone, but we want to retain our independence. Meeting someone has become particularly problematic. Increasingly, we tend to fall back on our defences. But meeting someone always involves an element of danger because we have to open up to others. There cannot be any commitment to love unless the old self is put to death. Sophie cannot get used to this idea.[1] No sooner has she embarked upon a relationship than she feels ill at ease and thinks only of running away from it: 'I had to get away after five minutes. It was a general panic. Run! Run away, run away, as fast as you can.'

Unless we are swept off our feet, meeting someone now involves contradictory emotions. It also means that we have to do ourselves some violence. Knowing how to let go (leave the old self behind)

[1] I interviewed Sophie for *Premier Matin* (Kaufmann 2002).

has become an especially difficult art. And if we do cut ourselves loose, we may well be in for a big disappointment. You tell me, Isolde, that your relationship was miserable. A lot of women feel that way when the man who looked so attractive turns into someone who just wants to watch the football on television. They have the uncomfortable feeling that they no longer exist in their own right and that their relationship is dead. Indeed, that is their reason for seeking a divorce (Francescato 1992). In some cases, the converse is true: the relationship is far from dead but takes the form of permanent guerrilla warfare. But a couple who can avoid these pitfalls has one incomparable advantage: a pact based upon a special recognition.

THERE IS MORE TO LOVE THAN LOVE

The huge need for love that is now being expressed everywhere often masks a demand for recognition. 'We cannot live without this recognition because it is the basis for our dignity and self-esteem' (Caillé 2004: 5). When we are loved, we feel that we exist (Todorov 2001 [1995]). Being loved by a partner makes up for the lack of recognition. That lack is a structural product of our society because it is a system of generalized competition in which everyone is trying to outdo everyone else. We have to be successful in every sphere because this is an immense competition in which everything – the way we eat, the way we take our holidays – is liable to be judged. We used to go on holiday to relax or to have a good time. We now have to make a success of our holidays, and have a fantastic story to tell our friends and colleagues when we get home. And it is the opinion of close friends and relatives that counts for most (and that is a problem in itself). They are the ones we have to beat, even though we love them dearly. If we have children, they have to do better at school than their children. We have to make a success of our holidays. We even have to make sure we get the weather forecast right! We have to love our friends, but we also have to do better than them. And that is a real tragedy, especially as we all judge each other on the basis of our own criteria. And those criteria mean that we justify our existence by denigrating the existence of other people. So-and-so goes on camping holidays in order to save money, but he talks about being in touch with nature and about the human warmth of his fellow campers because he wants to put down his relatives or neighbours. They spend their holidays in luxury high-rise hotels built of concrete and don't know how to enjoy the important things in life. We work on the basis of criteria that give us good marks and give other people bad marks. And so our self-esteem gets lower and lower as our kindly but critical neighbours look on. The demand for recognition masks a huge – and growing – need for love.

This structural deficit reflects the way everyone rates everyone else, but there is another major problem: recognition is not something cumulative in the sense that a pile of bricks is cumulative. On the contrary, it is often the product of a process of subtraction. We all belong to many different groups and display different aspects of our identity when we are with them: when we are with our families, we are not what we are when we are at the sports club, in a union meeting, or at a meeting of the movie-poster collectors' club. When we are in those circles, we are recognized as someone who exists and who matters, but we always 'matter' in a particular way. It is when the circles overlap that the problems begin: when it comes to recognition, what we win on the roundabouts, we lose on the swings. Compartmentalizing our lives is one way to prevent that happening, but doing so is often neither easy nor desirable. So we have to create hierarchies, and choose some circles and not others, should they overlap. And that is where relationships begin to matter. Once we are in a relationship, the relationship has to take priority, no matter which social circles we move in. There is no escaping that golden rule. This also explains why commitment has become so difficult, and why it can even damage our individual sense of identity. It upsets the way we construct our personalities as others look on. Commitment leads to the creation of privileged circles. In the other circles in which we move, recognition is either friendly or tinged with esteem, but inside our privileged circle it is tinged with love. Unlike those circles, this one is based upon a mutual admiration pact. We touch and caress each other: this is not the movie-posters collectors' club. There is no doubt about that.

THE GOLDEN RULE OF RELATIONSHIPS

The conflicts that arise between couples and other circles within the family are the best example. The family is often seen as a site of consensual affection. And there is a lot of love within the family, but it inevitably comes into conflict with other forms of love. We seek recognition for two reasons: to improve our self-esteem, and to confirm our individual sense of identity. Depending on which we role we are playing at any given moment (son or daughter, brother or sister, husband or wife . . .), different facets of our personality are recognized. We constantly try to erase these differences, to avoid the issue and to smooth things over, and to pretend that they are only minor problems. They are in fact major problems, and they will not go away. In the very early stages of a marriage, there is often a conflict between the parents (who have their own image of their child) and the new member of the family, who is using married life to construct a partner who may look very different. As a general rule, the family resents this but grudgingly admits that the relationship has to take priority. But after ten or twenty years of married life, even a minor family squabble can become an outlet for criticisms that have never before been voiced in so many words.

Fortunately, the golden rule of relationships is there to limit the damage by establishing a hierarchy: no matter how much you love your parents, your partner has to come first. And that implies that we have to support and collude with our partners. In our day-to-day conversations, we arrive at subtle compromises, but that requires a great deal of diplomacy. When we are with other members of the family, this delicate conjugal alchemy does not always work. Being in close contact with them can reactivate other facets of the identity of one or other of the partners as he or she reverts to being a son or a daughter, a brother or a sister. Isabelle describes what can happen next: 'What gets on everyone's nerves is when someone in the family attacks and our dear partner acts as if nothing has happened, or even springs to the defence of their clan' (Kaufmann 2009 [2007]: 121). She feels that she has to act as a referee. This takes a lot of skill, as she also has to remain open and attentive to her own partner's needs. It also means being able to improvise the constantly changing conditions required to maintain a united front. But both partners' sensibilities may shift when they are with their respective families. Isabelle keeps a watchful eye on her husband, and does not really take his words at face value: even though he claims (in the privacy of their private conversations) not to think too much of his sister and to consider her 'useless' in all sorts of ways, he changes his tune dramatically when Isabelle oversteps the line and pours insults on 'that slut' . . .

> I've got one sister-in-law who I always refer to as 'that slut' or something even fruitier, but I know that my darling doesn't have a particularly high opinion of her, and thinks she's pretty useless in many ways. Basically it's become a sort of private joke between us with him pretending to be offended and me laying it on even thicker. But that doesn't stop me from going with him to spend New Year with 'that slut', complaining the whole way about how much I hate it, how she doesn't even have a job yet still insists that everyone brings some food, that it's disgraceful, that I've never seen anything like it, and so on blah, blah, blah . . . In fact I get it all off my chest so that when I come face to face with the slut herself I can be perfectly pleasant and good tempered. By moaning about it beforehand, I manage to preserve some semblance of respectable hypocrisy which is really important. If you said exactly what you thought about everyone, all those family meals would end up in complete punch-ups. (Kaufmann 2009 [2007]: 121–2)

COMFORT AND SOLACE

Being part of a couple is incredibly complicated. Once we get over the emotional shock of meeting someone, we build a strange little world for two. It is a world that is based upon shared values and that is cut off from the rest of the big wide world. And inside this little world, each partner is also in his or her own world and exchanges all sorts of things with his or her partner: money, the things they do for each other, words, emotions and gestures, some gentle and some not so gentle. The principle behind these exchanges is that, if we strike the right balance, both partners will, on the whole, feel satisfied. Doing the washing-up alone yet again while your partner is watching television does not matter if, a moment later, just a few kind words are enough to make you forget that momentary unpleasantness. We often chalk up our partner's good and bad points, but we do not do so all the time, thanks to the golden rule that binds couples together despite the vicissitudes of everyday life. Relationships work on the basis of functional logics that are very different but that do mesh. One is the logic behind the way we experience the relationship in our actual lives (the contradiction is that this logic is inconsistent: outbursts of passion alternate with cold calculation). The other logic is a matter of principle, an absolute a priori that makes its presence felt no matter what happens in our day-to-day lives. It is based upon the golden rule of mutual trust and reciprocal recognition. No matter what our partner says or does, he or she is right and deserves our admiration. A partner is an unconditional supporter and an absolute fan.

In the course of my research on family meals, I found that one of their recurrent topics of conversation is 'And how was your day?' These stories are full of injustices (unfairness, bullying) and perceived insults, especially at work. They take the form of very repetitive serials, and the figure of the baddy often makes recurrent appearances ('He did it to me again', 'She said it again'). 'He' or 'she' is a negative hero who triggers bad emotions that have been stored up and which now have to be released. The partner acts as a therapist who lends a sympathetic ear, provides active support ('He's disgusting', 'Yes, she's a real pain') and supplies an outlet for the accumulated stress. He or she is the sympathetic listener and the shoulder to cry on that we need so much.

Being part of a couple means being part of something that is both very simple and very important: it is a source of comfort and solace. That it may also be exciting because of the feelings that are exchanged is of secondary importance. The world in which we live is very harsh because it is based upon generalized competition and because its dominant model is that of the cold, calculating individual. It is as though we were always leading a double life, with each of our lives being dominated by a different model for the individual. The public sphere is the realm of a rational individualism which is, alas, all too often reduced to meaning calculating selfishness. There is, however, no way of escaping that rationality, as it is also the basis for democratic citizenship. The problem is that it is devoid of all feeling, whereas life is all about feelings. Hence the need for a different life, for a private sphere that can provide comfort and solace, and for a realm that is ruled by a very different kind of individual. When I looked at the apparently banal question of how we feel when we go into someone's home, I was struck by how many people felt that they were entering a different world when they crossed the threshold. They immediately felt that they were entering a warm environment, and that feeling had nothing to do with the actual temperature. 'Home' creates individuality by following different rules (Pezeu-Massabuau 2003; Serfaty-Garzon 2003), but a homely atmosphere also has something to do with love.

A PARTICULAR UNIVERSALISM

We cannot live without love. It is quite impossible. And it is now even more impossible than ever before to do so. We cannot live without all the very different forms of love that have been handed down to us by centuries of history. And the first of them is the love that forges an unconditional bond. This idea has often cropped up in our story. It first appeared outside the family, in religious dreams of a society that could be ruled by our love for our fellow human beings. It also appeared in the Enlightenment ideal of universal benevolence and all the other virtues that supposedly reveal the basic humanity of human beings. And it appeared, finally, in the guides to married etiquette that cultivated the idea that we should adopt a charitable and generous attitude towards our partners. And it always takes the same form: it implies the adoption of a systematic principle that claims to be universal, and that often derives from the Christian notion of *agape* – we must love our neighbours as ourselves, and we must love all our neighbours, no matter how awful they may be. We have to love both God and earthworms, and we even have to love our enemies. We therefore have to love our partner in his or her 'most contingent and most negative particularities' (Bourdieu 2001 [1998]: 110).

The golden rule (the pact of privileged recognition and mutual support) is directly and obviously descended from these various expressions of a single principle. It may derive directly from them, but it also profoundly alters the way they work. The first thing we have to note is that the golden rule means that, after so many failures, love's utopia has at last become a reality. It is certainly a reality within the secondary spheres that provide us with comfort and solace. And perhaps love's defeat has been confined to the social sphere. Elsewhere, it continues to gain ground. Whilst the world talks of nothing but competition, assessments and calculations, millions and millions of couples function as utopian micro-communities that are bound together by a new kind of *agape*. After so many fruitless attempts, love's utopias have at last become a reality, albeit in a very discreet fashion; they certainly do not take the revolutionary form one might have imagined.

The most curious thing about this recent shift in the way that we feel is that a new inversion has taken place. Christian *agape* and secular benevolence both claimed to be universal virtues. Passion, in contrast, focuses on one person or one idea, and cuts it off from the world at large. The paradox is that a 'universal' value now functions within individual private worlds. But the principle remains the same: we love our partners, no matter what they do or say. The difference is that the principle is now exclusive and applies to only one person.

This individualized universalism is a product of history, but it is not an archaic form; it is bound up with some very recent developments. This type of love appears to be positional: we love our partners because they are our partners. This is in a sense a love without qualities for a man or woman without qualities, but I cannot imagine anyone getting excited about that definition and it is true that it sounds less exciting than romantic passion. I suggest, however, that it would be a mistake to dismiss it too quickly, as it is of much greater import than it might seem. It is, for instance, significant that it should emerge at a time when the institution of marriage is being undermined. It is therefore not just an institutional effect, as it was for couples belonging to earlier generations. They were taught to love one another for life because there was no other solution. Marriage was for better or worse. If it proves to be for worse, the modern solution is divorce. The problematic has been inverted; it is now a very special form of love that guarantees the survival of the institution.

I would even go as far as saying that this form of love is more subversive than it might seem. In a society in which we are constantly being told to keep our analytic distance, to be unsparing in our assessments and remorseless in our criticisms, it teaches a rare wisdom that is very difficult to put into practice today. It quite simply teaches us to be with someone else.

THE QUEST FOR WELL-BEING

A conjugal *agape* enriched with mutual trust and recognition provides a foundation. It provides the elementary foundations on which we can build storeys of richer and more inventive feelings. And without those foundations, no building will stand up for very long.

These storeys all rise up towards the heaven of happiness and 'the happiness of giving happiness' (Bourdieu 2001 [1998]: 110). In the same way that some people once thirsted after the divine Light, we thirst after happiness, which has become the ultimate goal. We obviously thirst after happiness because the world is a hard place, because it is cold and aggressive and because the selfish individual model does not, to put it mildly, generate universal benevolence. But we also thirst after happiness because our autonomy forces us to do so, because we all have to find our own way in life, and because we have to believe in the story we are telling. We have to be consistent with ourselves, and that is not easy because the meaning of our day-to-day actions, and of our entire lives, constantly raises questions, gives rise to doubts and eludes us. Christophe André (2009) points out that the sensation of happiness is largely the product of the harmony that comes from the experience of a plenitude of meaning. It is not easy to feel happy when you are being persecuted by a boss who is screaming at you, or when your world is being torn apart by an adolescent crisis. Fortunately, there is a new way of being happy: we can accumulate 'pleasant states of mind' (André 2009: 375), or brief moments of happiness snatched in our drab everyday lives. The ideal solution would be to combine the two in such a way that our moments of happiness are part of a world that legitimates and extends them.

Conjugal *agape* provides the rudiments of this world, and moments of well-being can be grafted onto it. The quest for well-being has become the new frontier. We can forget about the vulgar comforts of the past. They were narrowly physical and objectively quantifiable. Well-being takes us on an endless quest, and as the very expression indicates to anyone who understands its meaning, it is a profoundly existential quest. The desire for well-being easily becomes an existential quest for the good, which is the concrete, tangible version of happiness. Happiness is the modern Grail, and it is, alas, always out of reach. Well-being is happiness in the here and now. We achieve it thanks to countless little pleasures, minor gestures and the most laughable objects. The new alchemy consists in transforming this dust into gold and scattering it everywhere, and in using scents, colours and gentle touches to delight the senses. Our five senses are gradually becoming more refined.

Studies in experimental psychology show that our eyes can now grasp the information contained in an image a fraction of a second more quickly than they could a few years ago (Sauvageot 1994). Our senses of hearing, taste, smell and touch are also becoming more refined. More important still, we are improving our ability to enjoy tiny sensations that we scarcely noticed in the past. Nothing is beneath contempt because anything can trigger a positive emotion. It might be a moment, a gesture or an object. It could be anything, no matter how trivial it may seem. It might even be a common-or-garden screwdriver.

DIY LOVE

You are going to be disappointed! I am going to talk about DIY and screwdrivers when I should be talking about love. Bear with me for a moment. This digression will show that love takes many different forms, and that it sometimes hides away where we least expect to find it. I discovered that in an earlier study of the meaning of cooking (Kaufmann 2010 [2005]). Cooking for the family is always an act of loving self-sacrifice, and it sometimes affords us the added pleasure of making other people happy. I accept that cooking is a more obvious example of love than DIY, but I have deliberately chosen the latter example. Daniel Miller (1998) rejects the essentialized conception that sees love as an abstract, ethereal entity, and demonstrates that it is also a product of the ordinary pragmatics of everyday life. An analysis of 'the material culture of love' (Miller 1998: 137) reveals some of the more unfamiliar parts of its mechanism. I am obviously not suggesting that we should reduce love to cooking, and still less to DIY, or that we should forget about the soft words, the cuddles or what goes on in bed. Cooking and DIY are not, on the other hand, separate domains, and what is going on here is probably not, in terms of love, as unimportant as it might seem. Thanks to the magic of cookery, love can take the very concrete form of peeling onions and kneading dough. And the DIY enthusiast who redecorates the entire house is establishing the preconditions for the happiness to come – with his hands.

Modernity has forgotten about hands. It is only interested in brains, and thinks that they are the only things that matter. But hands can bring about magical little syntheses because they make things we can actually touch. A few tools is all they need: a casserole, a spatula and a knife for the cook, and a hammer, a paintbrush and a screwdriver for the home decorator. That can be enough to change the world in which we love. It changes more than our internal décor, which is no more than an optical illusion. Day by day, our surroundings make us what we are. Families and relationships are made by hand.

DIY and decorating are increasingly popular hobbies. And more and more women are taking them up. When you are mixing concrete, you do not worry too much about the rest of your life: ontological problems are reduced to the reassuring materiality of a building site. Hammers, paintbrushes and screwdrivers quietly add meaning to our lives, day by day. And that meaning is new, shiny and spick and span; we can touch it. The DIY enthusiast who embarks upon this quiet quest for ordinary happiness then discovers that there is more than one dimension to his or her modest art. He or she is creating something that will last. Modern individuals are tormented because they know that they are mortal. And so they try to create an afterlife for themselves by leaving traces in the form of definite achievements that will, they hope, halt the passage of time. They write, draw and take photographs. The density of these things appears to be proportional to the weight of the raw materials, which might be metal, wood or stone. DIY products are meant to stand the test of time. And these personal creations are labours of love too. We make them for our loved ones, and we try to ensure that the moment of happiness that we share will be even more beautiful in the future. Love is made by hand too.

But that is not the point I was trying to make. I was trying to make a point about screwdrivers. You remember what the old screwdrivers were like (it isn't that long ago). DIY was still very much a male pastime, still betrayed its origins in the world of work, and was still dominated by the idea of manly strength. The screwdrivers of the day had grooved wooden handles with sharp edges, and it hurt to use them if you did not have calloused hands. And they had negative associations; 'screwing someone' did not have nice connotations.

Screwdrivers have changed since then. The new demand for 'soft' tools means that they now sport handles made from polymers and are astonishingly easy to use. The rough edges are a thing of the past, and driving home a screw can actually produce a pleasant feeling in the palm of the hand. You might object that it is only a passing, and therefore insignificant, feeling, and you would be right to say that. Yes, it is minuscule, you will tell me: it is microscopic and therefore trivial. But screwdrivers were never meant to be a source of pleasure. They are just means to an end, and they help to create the pre-conditions for our well-being. It therefore comes as something of a surprise to find that these eminently banal actions can now give rise to a sensation that is far from unpleasant.

The Density of Love

The solid foundations of conjugal *agape* can support many storeys of love. We build more and more storeys, and we build them higher and higher in a bid to reach the heavenly happiness we long for. The home is the classic setting for this slow build-up of ordinary love, which is why I use metaphors drawn from the building industry to describe it; my choice of the example of the screwdriver was not coincidental.

I could have chosen other, more obvious examples that do more to reveal the sensuality of domestic life and of loving-self-sacrifice. I could have talked about the personal pleasures we experience while watching a film on television or secretly nibbling at a square of chocolate. Or about cutting flowers in the garden, and then putting them into a vase. Or about playing music that fills the room with soft rhythms. Or about the joke that suddenly lightens the atmosphere. Or about the silent self-denial of the man (or more usually the woman) who sweeps the floor or does the washing up. The list is never-ending. Let me draw just a few conclusions. Although some of these examples have to do with personal pleasure, and some with generous acts of self-sacrifice, the dividing line between what appear to be very different categories is not clear-cut. Some personal pleasures can, of course, be real declarations of war. I saw many examples of this when I was working on couples' 'gripes' (Kaufmann 2009 [2007]: 55, 85). Robert, for instance, sits up late playing his video games while Eliza waits for him to come to bed in the forlorn hope that they will at last be able to talk to each other. She is well aware that staying glued to the screen is Robert's way of avoiding that intimacy. But when pleasures are part of a harmonious whole, they are just what we want: the group allows everyone to feel good and to experience pleasant sensations. And many personal pleasures do in fact impact upon the couple or family by helping them to forge stronger bonds. Playing a musical instrument for one's own amusement also gives pleasure to other people (provided that they like that sort of thing). The starting point for the flower arrangement may well have an individual wish to be creative; the joke may be a product of a desire for applause. That does not alter the fact that they also add more storeys to the house of little pleasures. This time, they are sensual storeys: the music is soothing, the flower arrangement is a visual delight, and the laughter is a joy. They are also sentimental stages because they reveal an active desire for a newly inventive commitment.

Generous acts of self-sacrifice, in contrast, are not meant to be a source of personal pleasure. They are gifts of love because we make them even when the work involved is a pain. Domestic activities are good symbols of the discreet love that quietly enriches *agape* and adds to its material density. And yet, they can give rise to countless pleasant feelings – if only that of the satisfaction of having done one's duty – despite the fact they are tiring, and sometimes even tiresome. And the most pleasant aspects of these discreet sensations have to do with love. It takes a long time to shell a kilo of green beans, but the family will have a good meal and may even enjoy the pleasures of the table. Ironing children's clothes takes a long time, but the way our hands caress the smooth, warm fabric is a reminder of other caresses.

THE ECOLOGY OF GENTLENESS

The golden rule is just the base on which we build our house. It is day-to-day life that gives love its density and materiality. Pots and pans, flower arrangements and screwdrivers all add to its density. There are couples whose domesticated love is unemotional in style, even though it is strong, but there are fewer and fewer of them. That is because the idea that gentleness and tenderness should be erected into a system is becoming more and more widespread.

The idea of gentleness is not really new. As we have seen, it was there in the secular nature cults of the past (expressing it was the main function of those bucolic landscapes). And the idea of tenderness is not really new either. As we have seen, all the etiquette books of the eighteenth century talked about it and saw it as the basic characteristic of any relationship. What is new is the way that both ideas have been systematized. As tenderness leads to greater tenderness, and gentleness to greater gentleness, a veritable ecology of emotional warmth is taking shape. It is being promoted by the institutions and professionals – the journalists, psychologists, marriage-guidance counsellors and magistrates – who have to deal with couples whose relationships are in crisis. A 'good divorce' model ('for the sake of the children') has recently been developed. Whilst the new art of divorce may not lead to a peaceful separation, it at least does away with the screaming rows. This is obviously not straightforward. Even so, divorces are beginning to look more and more like that model, and the peaceful handling of serious conflicts does impact upon more banal conflicts. In my study of couples' gripes, I was struck by how much inventiveness couples put into defusing their disputes. They can be incredibly clever about this. Even though – for reasons that cannot be explained here due to lack of space – there are now more and more reasons to become angry even without our partners, married life has not become a living hell, and this is mainly because we all want it to be gentle.

This desire is not restricted to couples, as is obvious from the fashion for massage and other spa treatments. We need to be touched, both literally and metaphorically. Being touched calms us down and provides us with a refuge and an escape from a harsh world. We need cuddles. Couples can no longer afford to be just a source of mutual comfort and solace; they have to learn to be loving, to touch one another and to go on developing new and more sophisticated forms of tenderness and gentleness. When we reach this point, the bricks I quietly accumulated to build my domesticated love obviously begin to look somewhat inadequate. We need more intensity, if not more surprises. We have to get beyond well-being: we have to discover pleasure.

Most couples have ritualized times and places that they set aside for pleasure. These rituals are intense and cannot be missed: no excuses are acceptable. So-called secondary pleasures such as meals can be very intense. Eating together is a ritual that it is much more intimate than it might seem, especially when we talk about the very carnal pleasures we are enjoying as we eat. But the most important ritual of all is obviously not usually celebrated over a meal. It usually takes place in bed, and sexual pleasure is a pleasure unlike any other. It is more exciting and more intimate because it feeds upon a desire that cannot be compared with other desires. Both the biology of the emotions and conjugal symbolism contribute to this. Studies show, for example, that many women derive no pleasure from penetration but still want to be penetrated. This is because sexuality symbolizes the reality of married life, and because the absence of sexuality signals that the relationship is in serious trouble. Sexual difficulties also signal that something is wrong. Problems that were once tolerable are becoming harder and harder to put up with because having sexual relations is the most intense moment in the new quest for happiness. This is when expectations are highest (Brenot 2001). Assuming that an obsession with performance and a selfish concentration upon one's own pleasure do not interfere, shared pleasure can be so intense that it leads to the enchanted moments I will be talking about below. It should, however, be remembered that, whilst it is more immediately perceptible, pleasure is not usually 'better than' well-being, which is the concrete embodiment of happiness. Technical prowess is no guarantee that the sex will be good.

Ordinary Harmony

I do not have a lot to say about sex because that is one of the aspects of conjugal love that is, paradoxically, talked about most often.[2] Others, in contrast, go almost unnoticed. Sentimentality is still denigrated, just as it was a hundred years ago. And this is especially true when it has the modest appearance of something that is simply part of the social density of the 'texture' of married life (Martuccelli 2005).

The aesthetic pleasure we derive from the most ordinary aspects of our day-to-day lives is a good example of how even restrained

[2] This does not mean that we now understand the meaning of sexuality. I hope to develop this theme further in future.

feelings can contribute to the growth of conjugal love. Sharing the beauty that emanates from a sound, the line of a drawing, or a piece of fabric gives us a moment's grace that both brings us closer together and heightens our pleasure. But as Sofian Beldjerd's detailed analysis (2008) demonstrates, the work that has to go into creating these fragments of the domestic universe is complex. Most households gradually accumulate a collection of odds and ends that were bought at different times and for very different reasons by one or other of the partners. All these bits and pieces represent a serious challenge to anyone who is planning to redecorate the whole house. Some of them have become invisible points of reference for functional activities, whilst others are mainly of aesthetic interest. Some are a source of pleasure (the little picture that was brought back from a far-away country), whilst others are quite the opposite (Aunt Yvette's old armchair, which is very comfortable but in such a dreadful state). The people Beldjerd interviewed agonized over how to justify these choices. Was there any overall sense of style and, if so, what was it? The heterogeneity of the objects concerned was so great that no one could come up with a coherent explanation of why they were important. Specific styles, concepts and ideas were of secondary importance. All that mattered was the 'feeling' that came from the indefinable 'harmony' the couples sensed because it reflected the way they saw themselves. 'It's not necessarily a colour, a style or whatever else it might be that creates the harmony. It's something personal, and it stays with you', as Delphine put it (cited Beldjerd 2008: 161).

These contradictions cannot be resolved, and they are impossible to rationalize. Sofian Beledjerd therefore concludes that couples resolve them by adopting a 'neo-romantic stance'. And their solutions are surprisingly similar to the high romanticism analysed by Charles Taylor. They feel, for instance, that they can commune in some harmonious realm that exists outside the real world, and that it is because they share some intimate, mysterious feeling that they are living in this strange world. The way we perceive our surroundings becomes a tool that helps us to give us a sense of self-identity and our identity as a couple.

Although modern couples obviously do subscribe to this day-to-day neo-romanticism, it is not easy to see how it fits into my story. As we have already seen, my story is punctuated by a permanent clash between the two main forms of love: universal virtue and passionate revolt. I have also shown how what was a universal *agape* underwent a metamorphosis, was enriched in private life, and went on adding more storeys to the building as it pursued its goal of a well-being for two. This stage, however, is a stage unlike any other: it comes from a very different tradition that is hostile to love. This was obviously not the first metamorphosis to have affected love. The dangerous tumult of romanticism had already mutated into schmaltzy romance. And the sexuality that was once regarded as the work of the devil became part of a heavenly well-being that derived from Christian *agape*. This is obviously another example of the extreme fluidity of love, but it is the most astonishing example of all. One of romanticism's essential features is its tendency to burn its bridges behind it as it sets out to create a brand new world. The house of little pleasures, in contrast, is built on solid foundations, and it is a reassuring world in which we quietly accumulate possessions. Quite apart from the fact that the level of excitement generated by aesthetic harmony is so low that it is hardly noticeable, this romanticism is nothing more than a marginal effect, or one of the many clever expedients that we find in love. Today's romanticism is more total, more radical, and we have to look elsewhere for it.

THE ROMANTIC MOMENT

Our first meeting with the man or woman we love is a classic example. This is the romantic novel's classic theme, and it can take many different forms. It can take the form of a violent electric shock, or of a gentle and more gradual attraction. An image we have just glimpsed may suddenly turn into an icon of new faith, and libidinal energy may play a more active role in the desire process. The encounter may take place in one of the novel's traditional settings, or it may be the result of a more improbable and unlikely sequence of events. I will not go into these well-known elements in any great detail, but I will allow myself one brief comment. Over a period of several hundred years, the novel established a code defining what a truly romantic encounter should be like. It should obviously be love at first sight (Schurmans and Dominicé 1997). Although both later studies and contemporary novels show that things are often much more complicated than that (the emotions involved, for instance, are both strong and contradictory), this model of instant perfection still lingers in the mind (Martuccelli 2002), especially as it is closely related to the idea that everything is somehow pre-ordained. Cupid does not shoot his arrows at random, and the encounter has to be a blinding revelation. The idea that everything is pre-ordained is reinforced by the idea of 'love in a flash'; as I have already said, there are so many flashes going off everywhere that we should realize that the man we 'flash' upon is unlikely to be the One.

Initial encounters in fact take an extraordinary variety of different forms. It is very unusual for everything to be decided on the spot. It is only in the stories that we tell after the event that it was a case of 'one look is all it took'. So let's talk about these stories. The beautiful stories we tell ourselves were often already there in the form of obsessional dreams (Corcuff 2006); the story we concoct with the partner we have just met is all-important. Anthony Giddens (1992) notes that modern romanticism takes a narrative form: lovers use the stories that they dream up and tell each other to make their relationship look like a break with the past and to invent their future (which goes some way to explaining why their stories are so often embellished after the event). The encounter does not take the form of a single meeting; it consists of a series of episodes, and they are all important. They take in different settings, and involve a lot of different people (friends, family). Even when it is a case of love at first sight, the later episodes are essential, and they are pre-scripted.

Try to understand what I am saying. I am not suggesting that the encounter is less important than people say. Far from it. For the moment, I am just talking about the form it takes. When I was doing the research for my *Premier Matin* (Kaufmann 2002), I was struck by the number of times I heard people say: 'Well, you know, our story is a bit unusual.' The only unusual thing about it was that it did not conform to the model. The whole point is that none of these stories – or very few of them – correspond to the model. And the model has done a lot of damage, because it can give the impression that we have become embroiled in a cut-price love story. Worse still, it can discourage a couple from embarking upon a relationship if they believe that this stereotype is the key to falling in love. I remember the stories I was told when I was researching the romantic dreams of single women (Kaufmann

2009 [2007]). The women I spoke to would spend a lot of time putting on make-up in the almost physical certainty that tonight would be the night they would meet Him, then take a quick look around the room and know within 30 seconds that 'He's not here.' There had been no blinding flash of light, so he couldn't be Mr Right. When it comes to love, there can be no half-measures.

I mention this confusion as to the different forms the encounter can take because there is a danger that we will miss the important point. It is the impact of what happens during its first episodes that matters. And these days, what happens is often truly romantic. No matter what the usual definitions may tell us, true romanticism is not a question of style or a way of being poetic and sentimental. True romanticism means inventing a new world (which represents an ideal sentimentality and harmony) and rejecting the world that exists. We can tell when two people are in love by the way they whisper in one another's ear (Bozon 2005b) and swap secrets as they create their 'enchanted island' (Bourdieu 2001 [1998]: 110). Creating an enchanted isle implies that they also tear themselves away from something: both lovers have to abandon their old personal worlds. That, of course, is why the process is episodic: one by one, they break the ties that bind them to old friends, to habits, to certain objects, and to everything that made their lives what they once were. The effort that goes into this makes it difficult, if not painful, except when it is the emotional dynamic that motivates the romantic break with the past. Let us be quite clear as to the meaning of this. I have described how couples then establish all sorts of little rituals and feelings by inscribing them in material objects such as pots and pans, bunches of flowers and screwdrivers (all the floors of the house of little pleasures). Single people experience a similar density; their everyday lives have a density of their own but they experience in a more individual way. Falling in love with someone breaks those ties. The two lovers are under the strange impression that they are naked. They are walking on air in a somewhat unreal world that is unlike anything they have ever experienced. It feels as though their feet never touch the ground. Whole chapters of their personal memories have suddenly been erased because they have met someone. This is why they so often say that they feel weightless or that they are flying. This is, however, a transitional phase, as we cannot live for ever in a void or without all the roots that plunge deep into our normal lives and help us to construct our lives on a day-to-day basis. In subsequent episodes they imagine the new world they are going to build together, and that world comes into being much more quickly than one might think. It begins to emerge on the first morning; to their great surprise, the way they brush their teeth and spread their jam on their toast are just examples of the many markers that they put down in a materiality that is already becoming more dense.

As Ulrich Beck and Elisabeth Beck-Gernsheim (1995 [1990]) remark, love thus becomes a 'little utopia' that is built from the ground up. As the couple begin to enter a world in which they will have to handle many complex contradictions, this very special moment really does represent the romantic utopia of harmony. This is a complete but intangible harmony, and it is basically emotional. It represents a transition from one world to another. Two individuals leave behind their usual, familiar materiality, and are left to their own devices in a stripped-down inter-individual relationship. This is a very unusual experience and, logically enough, the joyous lightness and emotions that they feel are more intense and more vivid. For once, their bodies and their feelings are the only things that exist, and they take up their entire lives. For once, their surroundings are nothing more than surroundings, and they do not imprison life within their memories.

This is the complete antithesis of the house of little pleasures.

WHEN LOVE DIES

What I am trying to explain is at once well known and very difficult to understand in any real sense. We obviously know that we are carried away by passion; we have all experienced that. But something more complicated also happens: individuals are changed and reshaped by this experience. They undergo a structural change. Whereas they are normally weighed down by a past that sustains their memories and helps them find their way in their day-to-day lives, they become intoxicated by this existential lightness and discover to their delight that their relationship allows them to break free from it. This moment transforms both their identity (they realize that they know nothing about themselves and that they are willing to change) and their geometry (their skins become their only boundaries). The long history of the passions, which began with Manicheism, now becomes very important because it allows us to understand the radical nature of this transformation. True passion is a mystical uprooting, a negation of the world: the Light is the only source of truth, and the Light quivers with passion.

We often take a different view of the passions because we concentrate on only one feeling, as though it were an independent reality. We say that we are carried away by passion, completely so sometimes. It may feel wonderful, or it may feel like torture. And then, we say, it fades and we lapse back into our humdrum routines. We also say that if the relationship is to survive, the flame has to be tended. None of this is completely false, but it is so vague that it cannot really be true either. We cannot understand just what mechanisms are involved if we fail to make a distinction between the two forms of love that have come down to us from two very different traditions. Passion is a utopia, and, for a moment, our emotions turn it into a reality that is not of this world. It is inevitably doomed to die, at least in its original radical form, as it can survive only if it rebels against the world. Couples very quickly set about building a new world – often with considerable pleasure – and elaborate a shared culture that takes the material form of a style, rhythms, ways of doing things, and objects. The couple's second life has already begun, and this is where the other love – which has yet to be invented – becomes crucial. It will not grow of its own accord. There are couples who succeed in staying together simply because they share the same routine, the same life-style and the same way of doing things, and because objects that have become familiar have been transformed into points of reference. *Agape* puts life on a very different footing, especially when it is enriched by multiple expressions of a shared well-being. Too many analyses insist that there is an emotional pressure-drop once the heady days of passion are over. They fail to see that a very different love is emerging (or should be emerging). It is less demonstrative and less exciting, but it is deep, magnanimous and subtle. Conjugal tenderness can be unexpectedly strong, even in old age (Caradec 2004). Whereas passion is disruptive and allows us to experience an exhilarating lightness as the old world collapses, the house of little pleasures is part of this world, and it is sustained by the minor details of everyday life.

Relationships that peter out do not die because there is no passion left; they do so because there is not enough *agape*, because the couple concerned cannot establish the preconditions for a well-being that they can share.

Here I am talking about passion and happiness when your life is, you tell me my dear Isolde, 'really miserable'. I'm sorry to hear that. But I am trying to tell the story of how love became a happy experience and not that of marital difficulties – that would be another long story. Although we all dream of love, building a relationship has become an extraordinarily complex business. That is because we increasingly regard ourselves as autonomous individuals with our own life-styles and because we live in our own little worlds. We find that the disconcerting strangeness of the other gets in our way, and we begin to suffocate when the other becomes too invasive for our liking. As Pascal Duret's fine study (2007) shows, the way that routines develop over time has a remarkable effect. The couples who succeed in staying together for a long time are the couples that can constantly reinvent their mutual trust and share at least a few moments of happiness. Nothing could be less complicated when both partners are involved in a process of mutual self-sacrifice. And nothing could be more complicated when a grain of sand makes the happiness machine grind to a halt and when they both retreat into their private domains. There is no neutral: if the positive gears jam, they immediately put the engine into reverse and the house of well-being turns into a battleground. There may be a soundtrack, with screams and tears on every floor. Or it may be a silent movie, which is not much better given that one can, as you put it, die of boredom.

It becomes much easier to leave the old world behind when the heaven of married life turns into hell in this way. Using passion to negate the past is no longer a form of self-harm. It may even seem desirable because we are motivated by a desire to come back to life – or just to live, given that the relationship is dead. When things reach this point, women break off relationships because they want to have a life, and because they no longer want to be just a cog in a domestic machine that no longer has any meaning. 'I had the impression that I was just a piece of furniture; he walked past me without even seeing me', as Juliette put it (cited Martuccelli 2006: 187). What is unforgivable is the feeling of not being understood and of being invisible (Francescato 1992). Men are more likely to be motivated by an immediately physical desire (Francescato 1992). They feel that they have to prove something (Singly 2000), and are tormented by the idea of no longer being as young as they used to be. So you see, there is, I'm sorry to say, nothing unusual about your story. Even the 'younger model' is very typical.

The desire to experience a new passion, and to feel that they are alive thanks to that unusual experience, affects some men to such an extent that it takes over their lives. They cannot have enough passion. As soon as one relationship is over, they embark upon another, and they repeat the same pattern throughout their lives (Bozon 2005b), whilst other men quietly commit themselves to a long-term *agape*. But they still dream of a romantic escape from this world (Corcuff 2006). The only way for couples to confine that fantasy (which is sustained by novels, films and dreams) to the realm of the imaginary is to put their faith in mutual trust and a different type of loving logic, and to curl up in its warmth. And if they are very clever, that does not prevent them from enjoying a few moments of intensity.

LOVING TACTICS

Creating conjugal love is a never-ending task. As a rule, this is not something we do in separate spaces that exist outside our daily lives, or at specific times that we reserve for the purpose. On the contrary, conjugal love is something that is created by the smallest details of day-to-day life, and even by those that seem to have nothing at all to do with loving someone else. The way couples quarrel allows us to take a closer look at what is going on here. Violent anger is rather like a bad passion: it makes us forget the world around us and completely changes our identity in a flash (but does not result in any harmony). This appalling emotion destroys mutual trust and evicts the individual concerned from the house of little pleasures. As he very often realizes that this will not get him anywhere, he decides to go back to his happy home. But if the emotional break occurred very quickly, going back to his partner can prove to be very difficult. Their love – and it is much more of a living reality than one might imagine, even if the

relationship seems to be dormant – has been broken. The preconditions that made it possible therefore have to be re-established.
And that is a long, complex process that must begin at the bottom.
In the course of my research, I was able to observe countless
tactics, many of them very inventive, that couples use. They often
begin with minor adjustments that are simply designed to reduce
the emotional tension (spending time away from one's partner or
simply doing something else). Once that has been done, the real
work of love can begin. The idea is that you begin by taking the
first small step. And it is often a very small step that is taken in
the banal basement of the house of love. We take it in the hope
that our partner will notice. A woman might sweep the floor after
losing her temper because her partner forgot to put the bins out
yet again. In some circumstances, sweeping the floor can be a real
declaration of love. It can be a way of saying that she is in fact
willing to act in accordance with the logic of self-sacrifice, despite
the acerbic tone of their earlier exchanges. And then – and this
can sometimes mean much later – come the words, the tokens of
affection and the more obvious displays of love. These things are,
however, impossible unless some effort has already gone into
rebuilding the entire system of an ordinary love that has been
accumulated through familiarity. This involves real manual labour.
As I have already said, love can sometimes be made by hand. Even
when the hand is holding something as commonplace as a broom.

Very different tactics are sometimes used. Once the aggrieved
partner has calmed down, he or she may decide not to bother
with the complexities of starting anew, and may launch an openly
amorous attack that uses the vocabulary of romance. Romance is
used to compensate for the lack of *agape*. It is as though the
memory of the horrors she had recently lived through had been
erased, as though she had been uprooted, then projected into a
different emotional world. Melody gets very annoyed by the way
her husband greedily mops up his plate with big chunks of bread.
She points out that this is anything but an attractive habit (in her
view, having good manners is the key to being attractive), and it
actually comes close to making her feel sick. And yet she is still
in love with him because he is tall and handsome, and dresses very
well. And the way he looks deep into her eyes still reminds her of
the way things were when they first met. She gets over her irrita-
tion by clattering the plates as she does the washing-up, and then

tries to catch his eye. 'Then, when I look at him, I seek his eyes, looking for that old sparkle. It's as though that wipes the slate clean. And "I forget", until the next time' (Kaufmann 2009 [2007]: 185). Caroline does the same. Although she was very angry with Marc, the magic of love immediately makes her forget how annoyed she was with him: 'I am so lucky, I've got a man who is incredibly sensitive and who knows how to apologize if he's gone too far. And then when he says "You're right. I'll try harder", I just melt' (Kaufmann 2009 [2007]: 104).

Ann Swidler analyses the way couples constantly articulate the two registers of love (which she describes as 'prosaic-realistic' and 'mythic-romantic'). Choosing the romantic option erases the specificities of the situation, and even its most unpleasant features, by making our partner look like our only potential partner: 'The culture of romantic love . . . [hones] the capacity to identify one other person as *the* person whom one loves, and to know that this relationship is "it"' (Swidler 2001: 201). Romantic love is not open to discussion.

ENCHANTED INTERLUDES

It is obviously easier to operate on this register in times of conjugal peace. Doing so may even be a way of adding another floor to the house of well-being, and it may seem to be the floor that brings us closest to the Heaven of happiness. This seems perfectly logical, but this continuist vision raises certain problems. We are talking about passion, and passion is always a form of rebellion that rejects this world – which in this case means the house of little pleasures. How can we add a romantic top floor to a house when its foundations are being undermined? Only a new conjugal art can pull off that trick. And it is has to be a very subtle art.

The basic idea, which is not always easy to put into practice, is that, if we get it right, the old world will disappear, together with identities that are limed in their ordinary density. This is, however, no more than a temporary solution that opens a parenthesis. For just one moment, we experience a different life. We can escape from our normal world, and we can experience the lightness that comes from walking on air, provided that we do so in the full knowledge that normal life will then resume its course. It is all the easier to be daring when we know that it does not involve any long-term commitment.

Although these moments may come as a surprise, they are usually pre-programmed and highly ritualized. They form a parenthesis: we dream about them in advance, and we then dream about them after the event because of the way we remember them. When I was doing some research into family photos, I found that it is the special moments that everyone wants to immortalize. It is the special moments, and not ordinary life – even though that is more representative of the way we usually live – that give us the irresistible urge to press the button, rather as though we wanted to capture life at its most intense moment. The actual occasion may in fact be quite banal. I have already said something about meals, which – assuming that no clashes ruin the occasion – are usually experienced as moments of basic well-being. We are at peace within ourselves and with those around us because of the deep sensual satisfaction we enjoy at such moments. We often dream of being able to make the pleasure last, and of using pleasure to heighten the experience of being in love.

But there is a price to be paid; if we want to experience intensity, we have to leave our ordinary lives behind. That is the principle behind romanticism. Somehow or other, we have to succeed in escaping from the ordinary world and invent a new life for ourselves inside a bubble that is at once lighter and somewhat unreal. This is not always easy. Fortunately, there are substances (some are legal and others are illegal, but they all come with a government health warning) that help us to break loose, and that is what they were used for in the distant past. In many societies, alcohol was regarded as a divine beverage that allowed humans to commune with the gods. The Heaven of happiness has now taken the place of the gods. In my study of meals (Kaufmann 2010 [2005]), I found that many couples had adopted the ritual of 'a little drink before the meal' as a way of showing that they had stepped outside their day-to-day life together. It was their way of trying to commune with one another in a different dimension.

A 'little drink' does not really offer much scope for romanticism, even if there are candles and background music. Other breaks, and especially holidays, are much more significant. It is difficult to imagine the existential importance of holidays, or the extent to which a ruined holiday can mean marital disaster (Urbain 2008). Increasingly, the idea of a romantic break is the principle around which holidays are organized; the aim is to reinvent ourselves in a world that is so different that we cannot not reinvent ourselves. In the dream setting of an almost unreal world, we dress differently, speak differently and move differently. We inevitably feel lighter. And those who sell us our package tours are obviously well aware of what we expect. They also understand the extent to which we have revived the old utopia of the paradise island. Bougainville's readers would feel perfectly at home in a Club Meditérranée village. Provided that we have the money, we can take a comfortable mental break in perfect safety. In other circumstances, passion means taking considerable risks, or even dicing with death, as it did when romanticism was at its height. An exotic holiday is, of course, romanticism as romance. And there is a lot of emphasis on the symbols of romance (travel agents offer 'romantic' nights and meals, complete with sunsets, soft music, images of hearts, candles . . .). Despite all that, such holidays are a real break for those who can afford them. There is still something romantic about romance.

Romanticism also reveals social inequalities, as not everyone can afford these cosy enchanted interludes. For those who cannot, passion in the raw is the only escape from a normal life that does not have much going for it. Fortunately, raw passion is very powerful in emotional terms, even though it is not easy to control and can end in tragedy. (Those who are found guilty of crimes of passion find it easier to have 'mitigating circumstances' taken into account if the accused took the emotional law into his own hands because he was 'lacking in social legitimacy' (Gruel 1991: 70).)

There is obviously more to life than a drink before the meal and holidays. Other scenes of passion have more in common with the classic image of love. Sexuality is one. As I have said, sexuality takes pride of place in the house of well-being. But even though it is not 'better than' well-being, pleasure can take us even further. Intense pleasure obviously takes us out of ourselves. It helps us to reconstruct our identity and to forget about the usual density of our lives. At moment likes this, our bodies are all that we have. The bed becomes a miniature version of the forest where Tristan and Isolde enjoyed their exotic interlude. In a sense, sexuality is rather like an exotic holiday in that it makes it easier to get away from normal life. The current climate of sexual liberation, which means that talking about sexuality is nothing out of the ordinary, has now led to the astonishing situation in which some couples use sex to compensate for their inability to communicate in emotional terms and for their lack of well-being. Paradoxically, a flagging sexuality can be revived more easily than the complex web of marital relations and, if it is well handled, sexuality can be a form of emotional therapy.

RETURN OF THE (MINOR) PASSIONS

The way we share the activities we are passionate about provides the best example of how love can disrupt ordinary life: we share the same passion. The word 'passion', which derives from a distant and radical mysticism, has, surprisingly, become part of our everyday language and is used, after all its linguistic travels, to describe 'mere' leisure activities. We can be passionate about classical music or football, and we can have a real passion for our dog or for the roses in the garden (Bromberger 1998a). Although the things that trigger our passions may look pathetic to an outside observer, this usage is not in fact aberrant. No more so than the shift from romanticism to romance. All these minor passions are real passions, and they make it all the easier to forget about normal life in that there is something religious about this idolatry and in that they do trigger powerful emotions. They give us the impression that our centre of emotional gravity has shifted, and that we are living more intensely than we do in our normal lives.

From the conjugal point of view, a shared passion is ideal: the two of us should share the same passion, and our passion takes over our lives. A passion that is shared looks less like a temporary distraction (such as a holiday) than a different facet of our lives that exists parallel to ordinary life. This time, the break from ordinary life goes on and on, and there may be a lot of little footbridges leading to the house of little pleasures. Take the case of a passion for cooking, for roses or for interior decoration: the excitement and the thrills may not last, but they do provide moments of well-being. But what is ideal from the conjugal point of view is rarely ideal from the individual point of view (Singly 2000). Most passions, and especially the most exalted, are deeply personal. Our partner knows about them, may share them to a minor degree, and more or less puts up with them (the operative word is usually 'less'). Music fans, for instance, worship their idols with a fervour that generates a real emotional intensity, but in many cases they do not tell their partners just how intense it is. Christian Le Bart's analysis (2000) shows how difficult it is to move between these two worlds. The move from the ordinary world of the house of little pleasures to the world of passion is easy. Going back to ordinary life is much more difficult, and passion does nothing to enrich *agape*. On the contrary, the more intense and the more individual the passion, the more it tends to destroy little pleasures, just as it does in the classic love triangle. This makes the increasingly complex art of living with someone more difficult still. Partners cannot prevent one another from having personal passions: there is a huge need for them, and the need is growing. All they can do is to try to ensure that things do not get out of hand – or to demand some form of compensation if they do – to ensure that they do not remain too secret, to lay down some rules and to build bridges that lead to the house of little pleasures. The old war between these two forms of love is still raging.

Minor passions are not to be taken lightly, as they are signs of the important change that is taking place in today's society. They may seem ridiculous to a casual observer, but that is never the way they are lived. They take over our lives – which then become more intense, more complete and lighter – just as all the passions have always done. Their rise represents an enormous ocean and it is swamping the 'calculating individual' model. The irresistible rise of ordinary passions is one of the most modern forms of contemporary love, and one of its most powerful expressions. If we look at it from a historical point of view, passion has always welled up again, even when it was thought to be dead. Radical romanticism appears to have led nowhere, except perhaps to romance. And yet all sorts of different activities still allow us to break away in powerful style: everyone can now invent a little counter-world of their own, and it can be both intense and exciting. Music, for instance, can fill our lives, carry us away and allow us to bond with those who share the same passion (Lyard 2008). Such little worlds mark a radical break with ordinary life but, like romance, they appear to be risk-free and peaceful. It is only in emotional terms that they are tempestuous. Classic romance is losing its grip on us,[3] and it is being replaced by magazines or websites that allow today's friends to express their loyalties more easily. Life-enhancing passions are taking over the world. They are often playful and inventive, but they are also, and without realizing it, subversive. Love has experienced many failures, and has been victorious only in marginal and consolatory spheres, but the irresistible rise of the passions indicates that the desire for love is back with a vengeance.

Love may well be taking its revenge, but nothing is simple. As I have already explained at several points in my story, the fact that its various sentimental facets are magnificent has not prevented love from regularly failing in its bid to regulate society. It is too unstable, too composite and too emotional. Passion very quickly gets out of control and turns into its opposite. You have only to look at a football match to see how the joyful celebrations of those colourfully dressed supporters can turn into a vicious confrontation (Bromberger 1998b). Today's new passions are gentler, and have a class nature: they are the private domain of those who are comfortably well-off in both material and cultural terms. Without those indispensable supports and instruments, it is difficult for gentle passions to take shape, and they therefore flourish in much more restricted circles.

The poor, in contrast, do not have the same range of possibilities open to them, even though their need for recognition (which is basically a need for love) is much greater. Their bursts of passion therefore take a very different form. Young people living in run-down areas develop a 'you and me against the world' mentality that generates bad and dangerous emotions. It unleashes resentment, anger and hatred, and then creates a composite but ill-defined 'them'. The destitute find the mutual recognition that they need by inventing a little world of their own and rejecting the rest of the world, which comes to seem very far away and very confused. Their world is neither gently comforting nor playfully inventive; this is a harsh but highly structured world that has its

---

[3] It still retains a lot of influence; think, for instance, of the international impact of the Harlequin series of romances (Houel 1997; Péquignot 1991).

own code, its own language and its own culture. The little counter-world endures because it is based upon bad passions, and because the individual is trapped inside it.

When individuals are psychologically fragile or socially disadvantaged, there is a great danger that passion will destroy their autonomy as subjects. They are taken prisoner by their passions, which take over their whole lives. All over the world, we can see more and more explosions of individual passions. The individuals concerned die because they reinvent illusory religious or ethnic communities, and secessionist little worlds that are at war with scapegoats of their own making. The passions that carry us away can bring out either the best or the worst in us. That has, of course, always been the case. But this problem is now becoming more acute, as the collapse of the 'calculating individual' model gives the passions a much bigger social role.

FLANKING MANOEUVRES AND COUNTER-ATTACKS

We therefore have to be careful to keep our passions under control and to prevent them from degenerating into hatred or violence. The major remedy is well known. It consists in using the law and Reason as safeguards. They are regulatory instruments based upon clear, equitable principles and they can prevent our emotions from getting out of control. This brings us back to the rational individual model. Although it distances us from the world, introduces an unpleasant feeling of chilliness, and is often reduced to the selfish narrow-mindedness of petty calculations, there is no avoiding this model. The present situation is as follows: there is an irresistible desire for love all over the world because our lives are so harsh and so sterile. There is a desire for love in the form of *agape* – a virtue that can be either universal or privatized – and in the form of the passionate interludes that add spice to our lives. Unfortunately, love's political projects have always ended in failure, and it cannot act as a central regulator. Indeed, the more passionate forms of love can be highly dangerous. It is therefore doomed to go on spreading its influence, but only in peripheral spheres such as houses of well-being, minor passions and humanitarian activism. It attempts to outflank the

alternative model in which the individual regulates society from
the centre.

I would have liked to end my story here, as this is, in relative
terms, a happy ending. After centuries of failure, love appears to
be outflanking rational individualism, and that is as heartening as
it is unexpected. Unfortunately, things are not quite as simple as
that. Just as love begins its flanking manoeuvre, it comes under
attack in the centre. It comes under attack within, and at the very
moment when the romantic impulse should have been victorious.
There is no avoiding the rational individual model if we wish to
found democracy and justice, but the model is not content to play
its political role, important as it may be. Increasingly, it challenges
love's attempts to tell us how couples should behave and how we
choose our partners. We are all torn between two models. Some
want to be autonomous, rational individuals who later try to form
loving relationships on that basis. Others are more inclined to let
themselves go when they are carried away by love, even if it means
ceasing to exist as autonomous individuals. The outcome is that
our personalities are being structured in two different ways, and
that they are often gender-specific. As I discovered when I was
doing research for *Premier Matin* (Kaufmann 2002), men often
begin to feel that their lover's bed is a trap. In order to avoid being
smothered by kisses, some make a little trip to the bathroom,
whilst others gallantly go out to buy croissants. They need to keep
their distance, to have some space to themselves.

Critical rationality's increased hold over our private lives is part
of a broader trend that encourages us to be informed about everything and to question everything. It encourages us to manage our
lives by weighing up the pros and cons in every domain, rather as
though we were scientists working in a laboratory. There is obviously nothing wrong with this trend; the opportunity of using
knowledge to create a self opens up immense possibilities and is
a new and exciting challenge. The only problem is that this is not
how love works. It will never work this way. To make matters
worse, rationality is devoid of all feeling.

The outcome of the calculating individual's attacks on love's
traditional heartlands may vary, depending on the nature of the
bonds that are involved. The calculating individual has no impact,
or little impact, where children are concerned, but can have a
devastating impact where a partner is involved. As soon as the

little pleasures and magical interludes fail to live up to expectations, the bad marks begin to mount up, but we keep them to ourselves. Families therefore function in different ways, depending on whether they are child-centred or partner-centred, and love functions in different ways too. Children are a special case, a realm apart, and almost an enigma, especially when they have yet to display the first signs of autonomy and are still small babies.

FALLING IN LOVE AGAIN

Children are special even before they are born. Children are special when we first begin to dream of having a baby, when we begin to want a child. The decision to have a baby is not a calculated idea or a cut-and-dried project: this is a desire and, like all desires, it has a powerful and immediate emotional effect. Life seems to have so much to offer. The young parents in waiting are already living their dream and they see their life through pink and blue spectacles. Their emotional world is pink and blue, and it contrasts sharply with the greyness of everyday life. There are some underlying anxieties (Isn't there some risk? What will it really be like?), but they are deliriously happy as they imagine the world of happiness that will soon be theirs.

Merely looking at a cot or handling baby clothes has a magical effect. The young couple are falling in love all over again and the baby they are expecting makes them go weak at the knees. They are prepared to give up everything, to devote themselves body and soul; their baby is the only thing that matters to them. In a society in which everything (including one's partner) is up for discussion and open to criticism, their baby is an absolute value that cannot be questioned. Their baby gives their lives a new meaning, and that is all they want. The parents-to-be sense that they are becoming different, and that their lives will never be the same again. As soon as their baby is born, the flood of emotion overwhelms them and makes them shake all over. They know inside themselves that the upheaval is going to be even more complete than they imagined. They suddenly realize that they have changed completely. They forget all about the life they used to lead. The birth is a physical experience, even for dad, who did not have a baby inside him. He has been reborn, and he is acquiring a new identity.

But they have no time to think about all this. As soon as baby comes along ('He's so cute!', 'She's the most beautiful baby in the world!'), he plunges them into a whirl of frantic, non-stop activity. Domestic chaos begins to look like a real possibility, but they have to cope somehow. The house is suddenly full of new appliances (a baby alarm, a changing mat, a bottle-warmer . . .) and life becomes denser. They can't do things by halves. They are willing to make any sacrifice for the baby they worship. Although they are already doing a thousand things at once, the ideal of perfection makes them do even more. They have enough energy to move mountains, and nothing is too good for baby.

Of course they sometimes get depressed when they think of the carefree life they used to lead, and they do get very tired ('When am I going to enjoy the simple pleasure of getting a good night's sleep?'). And when the baby won't stop crying, voices are sometimes raised when the over-worked parents have their differences of opinion. But there is usually a fairy-tale ending to these episodes. Parents are very good at resolving their problems one by one and at remembering only the good times. Look at the photographs of baby in the family album. How often do you see a baby who is crying? Never: baby is always smiling. And babies are gorgeous. The bad times are quickly forgotten, and we remember only the good times, just as we do when we read a romance. And the hero of today's romance is a tiny Prince Charming.

THE LOTTERY OF FATE

For the poor partner, this commitment has a very different meaning. He is being secretly watched and rated, and then he is openly criticized when things turn nasty. As soon as the bad marks add up to what is deemed to be an unacceptable total, the idea of breaking up immediately suggests itself. But I would rather say more about how relationships begin, about how we meet and choose our partners. It is at this point that the calculating individual does most damage in our society. For established couples, the golden rule of mutual trust and moments of shared well-being (which are rarely what we dreamed they would be), discourage this continuous assessment: the bad marks can remain a secret, and they therefore have no noticeable effect. The density of marriage acts as a shock-absorber.

When we first meet someone, there is no shock-absorber. And the calculating individual can therefore inflict more damage. The only alternative to calculating coldness is, he thinks, the heat of passion. And we are frightened of passion. A minor passion that is well under control is pleasant and easy to deal with, but gambling one's whole future on the basis of an emotional impulse is a terrifying prospect. 'Love in a flash' can be a rich and intense experience, but when it involves a life-long commitment, it is not something to be trusted.

Some people think that they just have to put their trust in fate. It is as though everything was pre-ordained: all we have to do is wait for the spell to work its magic. There is nothing new about this idea. In Plato's *Symposium*, Aristophanes recounts the famous myth of the better half. We were cut in two on Zeus's orders, and ever since then we have only been half of something larger and more complete. We therefore have to find our better half before we can fully be ourselves. The belief that love is preordained was then given a new lease of life by Christianity; if love is divine, we cannot possibly have any doubts about our partners, and the idea of divorce is therefore inconceivable. Even though life has refuted it again and again, this belief still survives intact. It is a source of mental comfort, and it means that we do not have to confront the difficult alternatives (cold assessment or terrifying passion). In many cases, it has been cleverly converted into the idea of a non-accidental 'coincidence' that looks strangely like a destiny. The idea of a lottery goes back to the seventeenth century. 'Marriages are no longer made in heaven: the dominant theme today is the secular idea of a lottery' (Daumas 2004: 266). The lottery is depicted in nineteenth-century prints, where a figure sitting on top of a cloud represents Destiny (Beaumont-Maillet 1984). In the more pagan tradition, we see Cupid shooting his arrows. There is always some ambiguity about these 'coincidences': they are not coincidental, and they reveal a pre-ordained truth.

In my study of single women (Kaufmann 2008a [1999]) I saw the extent to which a revived version of this myth can be a source of psychological reassurance and comfort. There is no reason to go on doubting yourself: all you have to do is wait – as in *Sleeping*

Beauty. Unfortunately, real life is not like that: a prince (if there is such a thing) does not just come along and wake Sleeping Beauty with a kiss. The belief that love is pre-ordained – which is very much bound up with the idea that meeting Him or Her must be a blinding revelation – does a great deal of damage because it prevents anything from happening. We are reluctant to commit ourselves to any relationship at all because we have not met the man or woman of our life. In real life, meeting someone is always an uncertain business. We are uncertain about committing ourselves because we do not know if this is the right person, and so on. The problem is that we do not have a better half waiting for us somewhere: there are thousands of potential better halves out there. And it is because there are so many of them that the problem arises. We have countless potential partners. We might have a good time with one, and not such a good time with another, but we will be very different, depending on who we are with. Living with someone is like an experiment: our identity undergoes a profound mutation, and that completely transforms us. This is not a question to be taken lightly: this is probably the most important decision that we will take in our lives.

Calculating Love

We do not want to make any mistakes. And if we do not want to make mistakes, we inevitably have to evaluate, compare and judge. Given that the lottery of fate proves to have its limitations and that passion frightens us, the idea of a rational choice seems only logical. To be more specific, we say to ourselves that we need time to think, to sleep on it before we decide what life might be like with the candidate(s) we have chosen. We put together a file, so to speak. And if the answer seems to be 'yes', we hope that love will develop of its own accord. This is strangely reminiscent of the 'inclination' that was supposed to develop after an arranged marriage. It is as though we had gone back 300 years in time, the difference being that we now arrange our own marriages. But is that really the case? Specialist agencies have taken over what was once the role of the family. The old-fashioned marriage bureaux are also a thing of the past. We now use modern dating sites that match candidates on the basis of 'scientific' rules. They may not promise that we will find our illusory other half, as in Plato's day, but their filtering mechanisms considerably reduce the number of partners we have to choose from. It is the endless possibilities on offer (thousands, if not millions, of potential candidates) that pose the real problem, and it quickly becomes insoluble if we go too far down the road of calculating logic (Illouz 2007). I have already described how men can become pots of yoghurt. In the virtual hypermarkets that sell potential partners, the products waiting on the shelves try to appeal to the consumer. But we can be in for a lot of disappointments and let-downs, because human beings are not commodities like any others.

The disappointments have to do with the fact that it is very difficult to choose on the basis of a comparative evaluation. This is the difference between yoghurt and people. When we are in the dairy products section of the hypermarket, tiny emotional discharges make it easier for us to reach a decision without even being aware of what we are doing (Damasio 1995). Because we rate the products on offer so quickly, it is easy to fall in love with a yoghurt. But when we are choosing a partner, our whole future is at stake and we therefore stop to think. This checks our enthusiasm and makes it very difficult to reach a decision.

The commodification of love can also have perverse effects. Rationality is the lesser of two evils, the only problem being that it makes both choice and commitment more difficult. As in so many other domains, the rational individual is all too often reduced to being the market economy's narrowly calculating individual. Increasingly, the logic of consumerism is poisoning many aspects of private life (Bauman 2007), and this forces us to try to cobble together complex solutions that allow us to come to terms with attitudes towards love that have not, fortunately, completely disappeared (Zelizer 2005). How can a calculating individual – who is potentially a selfish individual – 'manage' love? It's like trying to use water to light a fire. And yet this is precisely what is beginning to happen. Some people obviously do find the partners they are looking for, but they will not do so unless they transcend themselves. They have to forget their old identities and reach out towards other people, just as they have to do when they fall in love. 'J', for example, does not imagine for one second that he might have to change:

> I am single and I surf the net to look at the dating sites. But I do
> not want to have children. I eat only organic food and I never eat
> meat. I don't own a mobile phone because I worry about the radia-
> tion, and I don't smoke. I'm 35, and I've had 0 hits. No one under-
> stands me. I know I can't live on my own, and this is killing me.[4]

In the new dating market that is now emerging, we all cling to
what we are, and make specific demands of the product we are
looking for. And this is especially true of people with money, as
the commodification of the search for a partner reveals some
major social inequalities.

BUYING YOUTH

Like all markets, the market in partners is now being globalized
on a large scale; love is being out-sourced too. And this has
increasingly perverse effects. I use this example to demonstrate
how the commodification of dating can lead to unacceptable
abuses. The internet is, for better or for worse, speeding up the
globalization of life-styles. I will be talking here mainly about the
worse, namely the commercial sites that now offer not just dates
but mail-order brides. This market is growing rapidly, and it is
very profitable. At first sight, this seems to be a fairly positive
development as it allows some people to escape their loneliness.
A closer analysis shows that it is based upon an unequal exchange
between North and South (which now includes Eastern Europe).[5]
Nicole Constable (2003) has drawn up a damning balance sheet
for the trade between the United States and Asia, and especially

---

[4] E-mail communication from 'J'.
[5] The categories of 'North' and 'South' are very approximate. It might
be more accurate to speak of 'dominant' and 'dominated' countries. And
besides, the position of some countries is changing – sometimes very
rapidly – irrespective of their geographical location. Within the space of
only a few years, Taiwan has become a major centre for the trade in
'mail-order brides'. The young brides (who are both beautiful and docile)
come mainly from mainland China and Vietnam. Specialist sub-markets
are also emerging: Korean men, for instance, like to marry young Chinese
women of Chinese origin.

the Philippines.[6] American men (meaning wealthy, white American men) are interested in a particular kind of women and have difficulty in finding them in their own country, which has, they say, been corrupted by feminism. They want old-style women who are good housekeepers (Scholes 2006), and who are docile. And, most important of all, they want women who are young and beautiful. What is being bought and sold is obvious: submissiveness, youth and beauty in exchange for money. Hence the expression 'mail-order brides'. This reversion to the old tradition of arranged marriages initially gave the marriage bureaux a new lease of life by allowing them to issue lists of beautiful young women to men who were only too happy to look at them, or by organizing 'romantic' trips to the recruitment areas. This form of marketing was a little too obvious, even shocking, and soon proved to have its limitations when it drew the attention of legislators to the dangers of people-trafficking. The trade in mail-order brides now takes a different form, and uses the internet in what appears to be a more open and fairer way. The structures of the men/women exchanges involved in fact remain exactly the same.[7] In Europe, the mail-order phenomenon was a slightly later development. The trade is now expanding rapidly, and it is mainly a trade between Eastern Europe and Africa (Draelants and Tatio Sah 2003). Geographical preferences are beginning to emerge, and they overlap with either linguistic affinities handed down from colonization or racial proximity (some men prefer a hint of exoticism, whilst others do not). But the underlying principle remains the same: submissiveness, beauty and youth in exchange for access to the western metropolis and money.

The newly globalized marriage market has huge potential, even though the promises that are made are rarely kept, and despite all

---

[6] In recent years, American men have become increasingly interested in women from Eastern Europe. In 2001, the US authorities issued 'fiancée visas' to 8,000 young women from Asia and to 5,000 from Russia, Ukraine and other countries in Eastern Europe. The visas are valid for 90 days. If they do marry, the women obtain 'permanent resident' status; if they do not, they are sent home.

[7] Slightly better-educated women from the South (and the East) are now becoming involved. But men in the North are still asking for precisely the same things: docility, beauty and youth.

the misunderstandings. Young women from the dominated countries are primarily interested in finding an escape from poverty. Some of them also dream of romance because their dreams are fuelled by the western media, and because the reality of married life in their own countries is much more brutal (Draelants and Tatio Sah 2003). Unfortunately, the cut-price fairy-tale prince all too often turns out to be a very ordinary frog. They come down to earth with a bump.

In the long term, the globalization of the dating market may have far-reaching implications. Western woman are already finding it difficult to find men who live up to their expectations. Men, for their part, may well be attracted to dynamic women, but they would rather have wives who do not make too many demands at home as they want a trouble-free married life. There is therefore a real danger that more and more men will turn to an international market where they can buy submissiveness, beauty and youth. They may well turn their backs on the over-qualified and independent women of the big cities of the North. In the meantime, men in the South will find it even more difficult to get a wife.

This is a very dangerous situation, both in private terms (the illusory belief that a marriage can be based on an employment contract) and in social and political terms. We need love more than ever before.

All's Well That Ends Well

I was really afraid that my story would have a sad ending. But the desire for love is so strong that it succeeds in flaring up again just when we thought it had been extinguished. My story may not really have a happy ending, but I can hold out some hope for the future.

It is always the same with love: it is defeated by a more effective mode of thought or a more regular organizational style, but it always lives to fight another day. And fortunately, that is what is happening today. As always, love is inventive, sly and subversive. It may not be ready to rule the world, but its creative plasticity can do wonders when it makes the most extreme situations a little more human.

I said earlier that *agape* (mutual trust and the house of little pleasures) was usually of no use when we first meet someone. It should be of no use because it is a product of something that we later build up together, namely the conjugal density that we gradually accumulate. When we first meet someone, it therefore does not exist. Given that we have learned from experience that destiny is no more than an illusion, this ought to mean that relationships must be based on either calculation (which leads us into a blind alley) or passion (which frightens us). Love, however, has another trick up its sleeve.

As we have seen, the contemporary art of conjugality is based largely upon both partners' ability to create the conditions that allow them to experience the joys of little pleasures. This is the new criterion: a good relationship depends upon our ability to feel good. How do we know that we will be able to feel good with the man or woman we have just met? We do not, but attempting to find out helps us to make up our minds. All we have to do is to trust our instincts. And to remember that our feelings are never simple: they are multiple and contradictory, and vary, depending on the circumstances that trigger them. This is, of course, a long-standing habit: intuition is an essential part of love. Net surfers who have learned to test out the people they meet on-line by stating that 'inner beauty is the only thing that counts' (Lardellier 2004: 195) will suddenly reject a potential partner at first sight. 'You can tell immediately', as Caroline puts it. That is not quite what I wanted to talk about. I don't want to talk about the first time we see someone, about the soft words, about the emotions that carry us away, or about the more intense pleasures that come later. Nor do I want to talk about the classic descriptions of how we fall in love. No, I want to talk about the banalities of everyday life, of the stupid little things that are the stuff of normal life. What does that have to do with love? I know that everyday life often becomes a stultifying routine, and that it can be the one thing that kills love. And yet, thanks to some wonderful alchemy, it can sometimes turn into pockets of well-being inside the house of little pleasures. What will our life together be like? That is the crucial issue. What will we feel in the course of our day-to-day lives, which will take up most of our existence? The first experiences we share give us some idea, even if they are microscopic.

People who meet for the first time today are carrying out a new kind of experiment in love. Whenever they are together, they try to work out what it is that makes them happy together. Every new context (doing the shopping together, organizing a weekend away . . .) gives them the opportunity to make specific discoveries. But the most decisive discoveries are those that have to do with the banal realities of day-to-day life, which is why a couple's first morning together is so important. The way they share the bathroom and the way they butter their toast supply thousands of clues about what will become the most repetitive actions of their future lives together. When one partner is unsure as to how those things will turn out, it is not unusual for them to surreptitiously watch their potential partner. They may even try to think in more systematic terms: is this the right one for me? Some of the people I spoke to told me that they found it very difficult to go on thinking in such rational terms. That, as it happens, is why they distanced themselves from what was going on by going to the bathroom or going out to buy croissants: they wanted to clear their heads. But even when they did try to think about what they were doing, the answers they came up with were very poor and confused: 'When we think, we are in two minds; when we feel, we have no doubts' (Sauvageot 2003). They therefore adopted a different approach. Inside their heads, they replayed images of what they had just experienced in a new attempt to test their feelings. The more palpable the well-being, the greater the desire to go on with the experiment. This is very far removed from the consumerist logic of the yoghurt pot partner. That is because it is our feelings that take the decision for us, as they should when we are talking about love. And because rating our partner is a secondary consideration. We are rating ourselves. We are rating the new self who has embarked upon a relationship that is already changing us – which goes to prove that we have come to terms with what we have to do (put our old life behind us), whereas consumers in the marriage market cling to their own points of reference and go on making the same demands.

You might say that this is not a very exciting prospect. And you may be thinking that I was lying when I promised you a happy ending. And it is true that this is not the same thing as meeting Rudolph Valentino in *The Sheikh*. But passion is still a possible alternative.[8] It may lead to disappointment, but it is an incomparably intense experience. I do not wish to set myself up as a judge, and I am not comparing passion with our ordinary little sensations. I am simply describing what is happening today: many people are afraid of violent passions that may get out of control. They want to experience the feeling of being in love, but they want to be in control of where they are going. My advice to them is that the micro-feelings technique is not to be despised. On the contrary, there is a lot to be learned from it. It is a lot better than cold, comparative evaluation because it remains within the register of love. And whilst the love concerned may well be discreet and modest, it is not without its subtlety and profundity. It is in search of truth and puts our lived experiences to the test, and it does so with great sophistication. And, as they accumulate, those experiences can build the house of little pleasures brick by brick.

[8] Isabelle Clair (2008) describes how, whilst most of the young people who live in the run-down estates on the edge of French cities prefer 'fun' and experiments in love that involve no commitment, others (and sometimes the same kids when they are a little older) prefer to break away from the group to build an emotional world for two. They are described – either ironically or admiringly – as 'lovers'. Le Gall (1999), for his part, points out that it is easier for these young people to fall in love if they can meet outside the world in which they usually move.

Conclusion

You asked me if anyone has ever tried to create a society centred upon love. I think I have at least been able to give you a few answers to that question. A lot of different attempts have been made to do so, and some of them were very impassioned. Most of them ended very badly. And yet, whilst they seemed to end in failure, they did leave their mark and then re-emerged in new forms. All, or almost all, these public failures turned into private successes and thus created a world apart that was ruled by *agape*. The *agape* that fed into the conjugal density of well-being, and the dark romanticism that triggered our explosive little passions are the main two examples.

There can be no appeal against the lessons of history: love was never meant to rule the world. Nothing can take the place of the clear, stable principles on which law and democracy are based. Of course, they are cold principles. This model for the individual is reductive and perhaps even mendacious, as it rules out anything to do with feelings and passions in order to build institutions that are based upon clear and stable principles. But I fail to see what the alternative might be. I do, on the other hand, know that this instrument of government can be used in very different ways. If we worship it, we end up believing that reality conforms to the model. This leads to disaster, as it is tantamount to denying the importance of the emotions. Alternatively, we can regard it as a model that has to remain a model or tool; it simplifies reality for the sake of convenience and disregards the emotions for the moment. In that case, we are convinced that real life has nothing to do with the model, and that the desire for humanity, a concern for others and a thirst for existential intensity are the most important things in the world.

I would go further still, and I am very afraid that I am going to disappoint a lot of people by saying that I do not see how we can replace the market economy by waving a magic wand. Attempts have been made to do so, and the least that can be said of them is that the results did not live up to expectations. It was not that easy for money to become central to the system, and Simmel and Marx himself have analysed why that was the case. Money is a universal equivalent and it promotes fluidification (Dubet 2009). It therefore frees individuals who were trapped into oppressive institutions. They paid a very high price for their emancipation: there was a huge increase in social inequalities, and the consumption of commodities seemed to be all there was to life. But we now have to spell it out quite clearly: the idea that money can be self-regulating has led us into a trap, and there is no escaping it.

LOVE AS SUBVERSION

That has to be the starting point for any utopia. The only possible strategy is to outflank this model, to launch a counter-attack from the periphery. This is by no means a poor man's strategy, and it does not mean that all we can do is provide a shoulder to cry on. It means that the work of subversion begins in the margins: love has to adopt guerrilla tactics. And it has begun to do so, even though we are not really aware of it. Soft words and kisses are a discreet form of resistance, and so too is the simple art of promoting well-being by building thousands of houses of little pleasures. We can build another world, and it will be a more affectionate world. We can build a new world thanks to the mad inventiveness and vital energy of new but gentle passions. Another world is possible, and it can be more exciting than this one. The magnanimity of a voluntary sector that refuses to accept the necessity of suffering and poverty shows us what can be done (Atlani-Duault 2009). We can build another world, and it will be a more human world.

Love's armies are already on the march. And perhaps the realization that they are on the march is the most important thing of all. We have to say to ourselves that, whilst we cannot dislodge the calculating individual model from the centre, we can encircle it. The hordes that surround it may not be very vindictive (we are talking about love, after all). Sometimes they wear masks, and they are not always in uniform (we are talking about guerrilla tactics), but they are very active and they are making progress. A utopia is probably gradually being built before our very eyes.

Being fully aware of this is equivalent to taking up arms and trying to invert our society's hierarchy of values. The fact that the calculating individual model is central to any form of regulation does not mean that we have to put it on a pedestal. On the contrary, we have to develop a way of thinking that makes allowances by making a distinction between the needs of the economy and the important things in life, as those things are the basis of any civilization. Of course we need management technicians. We have to accept that (even if it does make us seethe with anger), although it is difficult to see how we can prevent their wage-demands from becoming exorbitant. But a society that thinks of nothing but its level of GDP is quite simply unliveable. The economy has to be put in its place. The economy cannot found a civilization that is worthy of the name, and it will never be able to do so. Especially not if it relies upon its loathsome vision of the calculating individual. Despite the all-pervading cynicism (exemplified by the style of humour that is in vogue with the media), there is a huge desire for a more human world. It is biding its time and waiting for an opportunity to find expression and to reveal its potential generosity. It is trying to tell us that paying attention to other people is more important than re-establishing the profitability of our cash flow, that love – in all its forms – is the most beautiful thing in the world, and that the experience of passion is an extraordinary adventure. You were kind enough to mention something that is very dear to me: the passion for knowledge. I mean true knowledge, not the techno-science that has masqueraded as the real thing (Klein 2008). True knowledge is very similar to romantic passion in that it creates a scientifically based vision that allows us to discover things in a completely new way. We urgently need to be enthusiastic about the great passion for knowledge.

I am not forgetting culture, even though it is so despised these days. I am not forgetting the arts and all the other things that contribute to the wealth of a civilization. But now that I mention art, it has to be said that, unfortunately, even the most beautiful creative impulses do sometimes fall prey to the routine attractions of the market. Do we buy paintings because we have fallen passionately in love with them, because we enjoy looking at them, or because they represent a good investment? Many passions that could have become subversive have been recuperated by money, and money makes them part of its reductive regulatory system.

That is the greatest threat to love's revolution. It is on the march, and there is no resisting it, but the counter-revolution is lying in wait, and it is already undermining it from within. That is why I became somewhat annoyed when I was talking about the marriage market (and it has to be said that a hint of passion never did anyone any harm): it is invading a space that, more so than any other, should be the preserve of love. These are not just personal issues. The way we choose to embark upon our relationships (critical evaluation or emotional commitment) has major repercussions for society as a whole. Knowing how to surrender to our emotions is political.

Dear Isolde

Just a few more lines in reply to your more personal comments. 'In reply' is in fact putting it a little too strongly, as I have no practical solutions to offer. We all have our own feelings and our own dreams, and that is the way it should be. I am not a psychotherapist. I'm sorry, but this 'doctor' can't help you.

You tell me that you can fall in love at the drop of a hat. That is a very precious gift, even if it can play some nasty tricks on you from time to time. Not everyone is so lucky. There are people who have hearts of stone or

hearts that are as cold as death, and
we really do have to feel sorry for
them. Perhaps there is nothing more
beautiful than feelings that can get out
of control. There is something magical
about the incredible revolution that
they can trigger. They use the emotions
to create a world.

You can always put the damper on your
feelings later, especially when you are
caught in a 'really miserable' trap. It
seems to me that, if you want to know
where you stand, you would do better to
trust your instincts rather than your
intellect. And why break off a relationship when it begins with what are already
perceptible little pleasures? When happiness is there for the taking, it
doesn't do to ask too many questions.

And speaking of happiness, I think I owe you some
explanations.

SOME REMARKS ON HAPPINESS

This book set out to recount the curious history of love, and I
realize that its title might arouse expectations that far exceed my
modest abilities. Love can be a happy experience, but I am not
trying to supply recipes for happiness. Many other people are
trying to do that today, and they are rarely convincing. If there
was a recipe for happiness, we would have heard about it long
ago. Happiness is too subtle and too complex for that to be
the case, and happiness in love is even more subtle and more
complex.

The idea behind this book was to explain how we became
involved in today's great quest for happiness. That is a strange
and complex story. It began in the earliest societies, and with a
debate as to which values should structure society. An essential

mutation occurred in about the twelfth century, when individuals began to attempt to define the meaning of their lives for themselves. The individual who is, in theory, in charge of his own destiny had yet to emerge, and there were several different possible models. Love was one possibility: it promoted individualism and it freed individuals from the weight of tradition, especially when it took the form of passion. Unfortunately, that fine sentiment proved to be incapable of ruling the world. It is too emotionally unstable and uncontrollable. In its most intense form, it rejects the existing world. And to crown it all, the permanent war between the two forms of love means that no credible programme can ever be established.

Love was not up to the task, and so we saw a third character take the stage in a triumphal manner. He is not someone to be trifled with but, sadly, he is quite incapable of establishing any ethics. He is, however, good at managing society (whilst guaranteeing the individual's freedom of movement) because that is all he is interested in. We then witnessed his irresistible rise to power as he became more and more central to the workings of society, and as he also became more and more forbiddingly sad and cold. Now that calculating selfishness has become central to social life, we all do our best to discover worlds in which we can find some comfort and solace. And we dream of steadily improving our well-being as we pursue our quest for happiness. The immense need for happiness that is now being expressed is a direct product of this history.

Most of the techniques of happiness are bound up with love. The ecology of gentleness might, for instance, be defined as an affectionate *agape*. Love is one of our best guides as we pursue our quest for happiness, and our absolute ideal naturally takes the form of happy love. It is because we expect so much of love that it has, as we have seen, experienced such spectacular reversals: a gloomy Catharism gave way to a tame version of courtly love, and mystical romanticism turned into schmaltzy romance. Love could not resist the invitation to play the increasingly essential role of providing consolation in private places. It is generous with the cuddles that secretly cure the wounds inflicted upon us by the world. It may not make us happy, but it allows us to dream that we will find happiness one day.

Happiness Divided

It is a well-known fact that all happy couples resemble one another, and I could therefore break off my story here. But even when it has been recycled into the demand to make us happy, love cannot overcome its old divisions. And so *agape* becomes gentler, more affectionate and, if need be, more therapeutic. Passion tries to avoid wallowing in sorrow or melancholy (good passions are always joyous). But although *agape* and passion have both come to mean gentle manners, they do not, unfortunately, always get along. No one will be surprised to learn that they do not share the same conception of love. The old war between the two forms of love now takes the form of a conflict between two models for bliss, or between two forms of happiness.

The new art consists in overcoming these divisions, in moving from one form of happiness to the other without even thinking about it, and in pretending that there is only one form of happy love. This applies to both first dates and established couples. When we first meet someone, everything is mixed up inside our heads. Pleasant feelings associated with everyday well-being fuse with madly exciting crushes, as though they were basically the same but of different intensity. For couples who are already comfortably off in both material and mental terms, indulging in minor fantasies seems to add another floor to the house of little pleasures.

And yet *agape* and passion involve very different forms of calculation because they do not produce happiness in the same way. *Agape* is part and parcel of the real world, if only because that is where we try to find the truth when we meet someone. Quite apart from the fact that it is private and not universal, the *agape* that comes into play when we meet someone goes against the principle of systematic benevolence. That is because it helps us to come to a decision. For the moment, the goal is not to build a house of little pleasures together, but to decide if such a house can be built in the first place. And in order to decide that we have to trust our instincts, which are tested when we begin to share aspects of our day-to-day lives. If everything feels right, we can go on with the experiment and systematic benevolence does come into play. What was a relative and experimental *agape* then becomes a more general phenomenon.

Passionate emotions, in contrast, do not express any experiential truth. On the contrary, they arise because they wrench us away from the real world. They are inspired by sentimental dreams that invent a world which does not yet exist. And that is why there are so many mistakes and disappointments. There are disappointments when the dazzling flash fades and gives us a glimpse of ordinary life. This does not mean that there is something reprehensible about passion. Passion gives us the quasi-divine power to create a world, and we sometimes succeed in doing so. And the very fact of trying to do so is an adventure in itself, even if it does end in failure. The emotions simply do not serve the same function. In the case of the sentimental *agape* we feel when we are dating someone, our emotions tell us about its long-term viability by letting us know if our house of little pleasures is being built on solid foundations. When it comes to passion, the emotions are the weapons of revolt, and there is something dreamlike about them. Trying to combine exciting emotions and feelings that have more to do with everyday life (and which may tip the balance in favour of commitment) is tantamount to confusing two very different orders of reality. It becomes impossible to evaluate anything. I am not saying that love has to be rigorously evaluated. Nor am I saying that we have to be careful to keep the two forms of love separate or that we have to choose between *agape* and passion. On the contrary, the new art consists in combining the two. I am simply saying that the two registers relate to different forms of decision-making and that any attempt to blend the two can result in confusion. The experimental *agape* that comes into play when we begin to share our lives with someone submits our feelings to a quasi-scientific litmus test, even though it works on an intuitive basis. We are trying to find out whether we feel at ease with our new identities, and we therefore have no qualms about registering the slightest negative impressions. My study of the first mornings couples spend together (Kaufmann 2002) actually shows that it is not unusual for a couple to overdo this and to look for excuses in an attempt to avoid the discomfort and upheavals that are inevitable when we reach a biographical turning point. Passionate rebellions, in contrast, are based upon a systematic idealization that attempts to use our feelings to metamorphose the real, and to lead us into a new world that comes into being thanks to the idealizing gaze.

Juliette, whom I interviewed for *Premier Matin* (Kaufmann 2002) went over her first morning with Guillaume with a fine-tooth comb, picking up all his odd ways, including his strange habit of brushing his teeth in the shower. When she was with Romano, things were very different. She had really fallen for him, and waking up with him was like being in a fairy tale. Everything in the bedroom seemed to be singing for joy, and she remembered how the tree was in blossom and how she could hear the birds chirping. Two experiences, and two very different love-regimes. Colombine's experience began with the fairy tale. She had the impression that 'it was like being in a movie'. And then her eye was caught by objects that raised lots of doubts: she changed her commitment regime.

Testing the reality of feelings is not a job for passion. Passion tries to heighten our feelings in an attempt to create a new reality. Passion is a madcap adventure, and it still has mystical overtones. It does not care about the socks that have been left all over the place because it does not even see them. Experimental *agape* in contrast, makes a note of everything that offends the eye, but it obviously also records any positive impressions. The problem is that the accounts very quickly become muddled if we confuse the two registers.

Settled relationships can be analysed in precisely the same way. When we first meet someone, the important issue is that of how to come to a decision. We are implicitly asking ourselves whether a commitment to this man or woman can establish the preconditions for happiness. At a later stage in the relationship, the question becomes: how do we create that happiness? Once again, the two types of love relate to two kinds of accounting, two types of emotion, and two models of bliss. *Agape* builds the house of little pleasures brick by brick, thinks in the long term and thinks very responsibly. Because it takes abnegation and mutual trust as its starting point, these tranquil feelings of well-being are experienced as both an apotheosis and an achievement. When we have a passionate encounter, on the other hand, such tranquil sensations are at best a starting point for something more exciting, even if we have to say farewell to our normal life in order to increase the thrill. The *longue durée* gives way to the present, responsibility to the spirit of adventure, realism to an imaginative frenzy, and security to risk-taking.

THE LOVER

Plays about turtle doves trying to free themselves from the weight of tradition thanks to the virtues of love were the dramatist's stock-in-trade for hundreds of years. But once love had established its sovereignty over private life, the *théâtre de boulevard* theatre's classic triangle-schema of husband, wife and lover took over. It is still of contemporary relevance. Sadly, *agape* never gets beyond building the first storeys of what might otherwise become a happy house. A dull routine takes over and creates a miserable atmosphere: the promised happiness never materializes. And in today's climate, nothing could be more intolerable than a failure to be happy. The suffocating feeling becomes even worse when we try to imagine what our lives could have been like. At this point, just setting eyes on someone can be enough to reignite the spark and to set the heart beating.

Films, novels and song have said all there is to be said about the agonies of love. And yet it seems to me that not enough emphasis has been placed on the fact that these three characters are embodiments of very different forms of love. And this explains why anyone who is unfortunate enough to be in love has such difficulty in comparing them and deciding between them. It has, of course, often been emphasized that meeting someone for the first time is a powerful emotional experience because this is love in its nascent state. But the point is not just that it is nascent; it is also radically different, and all the more impassioned (it creates a new world) in that we dream of escaping the dreariness of our set routines. This experience can of course take many different forms. Our reluctance to give in to passion may simply reflect a fear of the unknown. In some cases, we are still bound by the contract of trust even though what we have built together is so dreary that it would make anyone weep. And sometimes – and this is presumably the most difficult dilemma of all – what is on offer is a passion and that might demolish a house of little pleasures that has already been built. This is why I am saying that the war between the two forms of love now inevitably takes the form of a war between two forms of happiness. The formula may seem paradoxical, but I do not think I am putting it too strongly. These antagonistic forms of happiness obviously cannot be cumulative. Too many contradictory offers of happiness usually lead to unhappiness. It is still difficult to love and to be happy at the same time.

A Strange Choice

An individual who is torn between these competing forms of love has to choose. If he or she gives emotions and sensations a free rein, anything that smacks of passion (as opposed to a mild *agape*) will win the day. Now, as we know, passion always looks beautiful in the short term, but its defining feature is that it has an uncertain future. That, of course, is part of its charm. To avoid repeated disappointments, we therefore have to decide what we feel and what we think after a period of level-headed reflection. The two forms of love are so different that they cannot be compared (they have to be judged on the basis of completely different criteria), but the strange and paradoxical thing about them is that we cannot tell which is which without turning to their common enemy, namely cold reason. I am not (or not yet) talking specifically about our third character (the cold, calculating individual). We can temper our need to reflect with an empathic generosity and sweeten it with affectionate attentions. It can be part of the project of being in control of one's own destiny that typifies advanced modernity in all its splendour. But what has entered love's sheepfold can easily turn out to be a wolf.

We probably cannot live any other way. We are condemned to live on a knife-edge. We have to be reflective, but at the same time we have to make sure that our calculations do not become so reductive that they make any loving self-sacrifice impossible. And in fact we get by quite well. We practice a sort of cognitive DIY that allows us to alternate between emotional impulsiveness (which gives us some idea of where passion might lead us), an intuitive decoding of ordinary pleasures and moments of truly critical scepticism. And we will go on getting by, provided that reason is not reduced to meaning narrow self-interest, which would drive us away from the other for good and destroy the bond between us.

KEYS TO BEING HAPPY

The paradox of love now revolves around the fact that there is an apparently simple solution to its incredible complexity: we have to learn to give in. This does not always work. Giving in can never guarantee that we will be happy. We can sacrifice ourselves again and again without getting anything in return. Some passions cause terrible suffering. From time to time (or on a different intellectual register), we therefore have to take a more analytical look at our lives, and make some decisions that are difficult because they are made when we are obviously not happy. But this critical distance must never be the most important factor – except in those extreme cases where our love really has become unliveable. The important thing is to know when to give in to love, and to go on and on knowing when to give in to it. And it does not matter whether we are talking about a gently reassuring *agape* or mad passion.

This may not guarantee us happiness, but doing the opposite (being selfish and calculating) is guaranteed to make us unhappy. Calculating selfishness creates hearts of stone. What is worse, it makes it impossible to be self-consistent. The calculating egoist constantly projects himself into alternatives that might prove interesting or that might improve his lot. He therefore transfers his identifications onto other selves that will, he believes, bring in more profit than the life he is currently leading. Now, he cannot have two identities at the same time and these flights into the imaginary detach him from his actual life by unleashing a latent dissatisfaction. This becomes a hellish spiral: the more he tries to ensure that he is happy, the less likely he is to find happiness. Love, in contrast, promotes a sense of fulfilment and self-presence. This is something of a paradox, as we do not go in search of love for its own sake and as we find it only when we are in the presence of the other. And everything that has ever been said about happiness leads one to the same conclusion. Happiness makes us reject selfishness, and it makes us available to others and to the world at large.

We began this book in the company of Monsieur de la Fontaine, and I will end it by stating the obvious: the best way to be happy is to love. Perhaps love is not so complicated after all.

A Note on Methodology

Who is sociology for? Is it for the researchers who try to deconstruct popular fallacies by coming up with new theoretical models? Or is it meant for all of us, now that we are asking countless questions about everything and need something to guide us in our search for knowledge? The answer to both these questions is an obvious 'yes', and that is why the science of sociology is more difficult to master than the science of chemistry or mathematics. And writing about sociology is especially difficult. Who are we writing for, and how should we be writing?

I have tried to do the impossible in this book. I have tried to write for the general public without making too many concessions when it comes to the content of my arguments. There is, I know, a danger that I will fail on both counts. Some will say that my supposedly light touch sometimes finds it difficult to keep its promises, and that all this talk of categories of representation or of creating counter-worlds gives them a headache. Others will say that my metaphorical-narrative style means that my arguments have no credibility and proves, should proof be needed, that I am not really a serious researcher. For the benefit of those who have followed my story, I would like to say that my choice of style was not determined solely by the needs of popularization. Of course I simplify things to an outrageous extent. I take a cavalier view of history, and I use significant anecdotes rather than amassing contradictory data. But how else can we approach the vast question of love, assuming that we wish at least to begin to understand it? Simplifying things whilst still observing the demands of science is much more difficult than relying upon cumulative descriptions or using a conventional jargon. I have, fortunately, had a lot of help, and my particular thanks are due to Jean-Christophe Tamisier, who was unsparing in his efforts to suggest some subtle improvements.

It is all too often forgotten that it is the ability to present an argument that is at the heart of the scientific approach, and not the ability to accumulate data (which can, on the contrary, kill theoretical arguments). And putting forward an argument in simple but lively terms is not beyond the bounds of the human imagination. If we can do that, a looser style ceases to be the opposite of scientific objectification: it is a way of making it accessible. Clifford Geertz attaches great importance to the art of writing science in a lively style, and that is why he prefers well-argued essays to 'systematic treatises' (Geertz 1993: 25) that do nothing to change the way we see things. Perhaps talking about theory is, like love, a utopian project that can become a reality. If it is, an argument that takes a narrative form may be its privileged means of expression.

In more general terms, I believe that researchers who explain their arguments, and link them together so as to bring out their central concepts, should have a concern for clarity. Rather than piling up layers of jargon and using obscure terminology in a bid to make their work look scientific, they should cut out everything that obscures their argument. They should try to put their arguments across as effectively as possible. That is the heart of living theory. It is obvious that not everything can be written in simple terms; when the links between concepts are complex they cannot be explained in snappy prose. But it is always possible to write more simply; sentences can be simplified, and the links between them can be made more subtle. And nor is writing in more personal terms against the rules. There is obviously a danger that we can go too far in that direction, that this can be a way of avoiding the need to construct our object more rigorously, of using facile allusions and metaphors to avoid the need for more systematic arguments. The main thing is that we must be in control of the processes of both research and writing.

Not all my books put forward arguments in narrative form. Some are based upon field work, and attempt to put forward their findings in a systematic way (the categories, classifications and typologies interrupt the narrative). Others attempt to outline a theoretical model, and are therefore more general and more abstract. The adoption of different perspectives (which means adopting the appropriate style), together with the variety of research topics, may disorient those who have read my earlier books, and may give the impression that there is no continuity between them. I do not share that view: there is a continuity. I have come up with a little game to make that clear: from time to time, I include a paragraph from one of my earlier books. The link indicates that there is a continuity. The reader who stumbles across one of these passages needs to be aware that the repetition is deliberate, and that it is an invitation to follow the link that leads to another book.

The decision to use a light touch (even though it is not as light as I might have wished) obviously rules out over-complex theoretical developments. I do not, for instance, make the connection with the 'double helix' theory that I develop in *Quand je est un autre* (Kaufmann 2008b). For those who wish to pursue this further, let me simply point out that my image of 'a long peaceful river' obviously relates to the first helix, or in other words to the socialization that accumulates a long-term memory that evolves slowly. The second helix describes the subjective rebellions and surprising reversals that punctuate my story. I point this connection out because one of the theses of *Quand je est un autre* is that if our analysis confuses processes relating to socialization with processes that had to do with subjective rebellions, we will fail to understand anything. We have to articulate the two carefully without confusing them.

The same applies to love. If we confuse the long, slow river of concrete behaviours with the surprisingly agitated and tumultuous dynamics of the history of categories or representation, we will not understand very much, and love will remain a mystery. This in fact helped to simplify my story, as I have concentrated on the way love is seen by those who tell us what love should be. It now remains for us to go more deeply into the way love is actually experienced. But, as La Fontaine puts it, 'I do not claim to explain everything here.'

Bibliography

Abel, Olivier (2006), 'La Fragilité conjugale', *Dialogue* 174: 85–94.

Alberoni, Francesco, (1982 [1979]), *Falling in Love and Loving*, trans. Lawrence Venuti, New York: Random House.

(1994), *Le Vol nuptial: l'imaginaire amoureux des femmes*, Paris: Pocket.

André, C. (2009), *Les Etats d'âme: un apprentissage de la sérénité*, Paris: Odile Jacob.

Atlani-Duault, L. (2009), *Au Bonheur des autres: anthropologie de l'aide humanitaire*, Paris: Armand Colin.

Augustine, St (1961 [387–8]), *Confessions*, trans. R.S. Pine-Coffin, Harmondsworth: Penguin.

Badinter, Elisabeth (1999), *Les Passions intellectuelles. I. Désir de gloire (1735–1751)*, Paris: Fayard.

(2002), *Les Passions intellectuelles. II. Exigence de dignité (1751–1762)*, Paris: Fayard.

(2005 [2003]), *Dead End Feminism*, trans. Julia Borossa, Cambridge: Polity.

(2007), *Les Passions intellectuelles. III. Volonté de pouvoir*, Paris: Fayard.

Barrère, A. and Martuccelli, D. (2009), *Le Roman comme laboratoire: de la connaissance littéraire à l'imagination sociologique*, Villeneuve d'Ascq: Presses universitaires du Septentrion.

Bauman, Zygmunt (2003), *Liquid Love: On the Frailty of Human Bonds*, Cambridge: Polity.

(2006), *Liquid Life*, Cambridge: Polity.

(2007), *Consuming Life*, Cambridge: Polity.

Beaumont-Maillet, Laure (1984), *La Guerre des sexes*, Paris: Albin Michel.

Beck, Ulrich and Beck-Gernsheim, Elisabeth (1995 [1990]), *The Normal Chaos of Love*, trans. Mark Ritter and Jane Wiebel, Cambridge: Polity.

Beldjerd, S. (2008), 'Goûts en movements: l'individu à l'épreuve des activités ordinaires dans les espaces du quotidien', Sociology thesis, Université Paris-Descartes.

Berger, Peter and Kellner, H. (1964), 'Marriage and the Construction of Reality: An Exercise in the Microsociology of Knowledge', *Diogenes* 46: 1–25.

Boissel, François (2007) [1789]), *Le Catéchisme du genre humain*, Toulon: Les Presses du Midi.

Bologne, J.-C. (1998), *Histoire du sentiment amoureux*, Paris: Flammarion.

Boltanski, Luc (1990), *L'Amour et la justice comme compétences: trois essais de sociologie de l'action*, Paris: Métailié.

Bottéro, J. (1987), *Mésopotamie, L'Ecriture, la raison et les dieux*, Paris: Gallimard.

Bougainville, L. A. de (1771), *Voyage autour du monde*, Paris.

Bourdieu, Pierre (2001 [1998]), *Masculine Domination*, trans. Peter Nice, Cambridge: Polity.

Boureau, A. (2005), 'L'Individu, sujet de vérité et suppôt de l'erreur: connaissance et dissidence dans le monde scolastique (ver 1270 – vers 1330)', in B. M. Bedos-Rezak and D. Iogna-Prat, eds., *L'Individu au Moyen Age*, Paris: Aubier.

Bozon, Michel (2001), 'Orientations intimes et construction de soi: pluralité et divergences dans les expressions de la sexualité', *Sociétés Contemporaines* 41–2: 11–40.

　(2005a), 'Littérature, sexualité et construction de soi: les écrivaines françaises du tournant du siècle face au déclin de l'amour romantique', *Australian Journal of French Studies*, 42, 1: 6–21.

　(2005b), 'Supplément à un post-scriptum de Pierre Bourdieu sur l'amour, ou peut-on faire une théorie de l'amour comme pratique?' in *Rencontres avec Pierre Bourdieu* (textes rassemblés par Gérard Mauger), Broissieux: Editions du Croquant: 591–602.

Brenot, P. (2001), *Inventer le couple*, Paris: Odile Jacob.

Bromberger, C., ed. (1998a), *Passions ordinaires: du match de football au concours de dictée*, Paris: Bayard.

　(1998b), *Football: la Bagatelle la plus sérieuse du monde*, Paris: Gallimard.

Brown, Peter (1988), *The Body and Society: Men, Women and Sexual Renunciation in Early Christianity* (ACL Lectures on the History of Religions), New York: Columbia University Press.

Cabet, Etienne (1845), *Voyage en Icarie*, Paris.

Caillé, A. (2000), *Anthropologie du don: le tiers paradigmatique*, Paris: Desclée de Brouwer.

(2004), 'Présentation', *Revue du MAUSS* 23 ('De la reconnaissance: don, identité, et estime de soi): 5–30.

(2009), *Théorie anti-utilitariste de l'action: fragments d'une sociologie générale*, Paris: La Découverte.

Caradec, V. (2004), *Vieiller après la retraite: approche sociologique du vieillissement*, Paris: PUF.

Carlin, C. (2003), 'La Métaphore du "Miroir du mariage" dans quelques traités catholiques', in D. Wetsel and F. Canovas, eds., *La Spiritualité / L'Epistolaire / Le Merveilleux ax Grand Siècle*, Tübingen: Gunter Narr Verlag.

Casey, J. (1985), 'Le Mariage clandestin en Andalousie à l'époque moderne', in A. Redondo, ed., *Amours légitimes – amours illégitimes en Espagne (XVIe – XVIIe siècles)*, Paris: Publications de la Sorbonne.

Castel, R. (1990), 'Le roman de la désaffiliation: à propos de Tristan et Iseut', *Le Débat* 61: 152–64.

(2002 [1995]), *From Manual Workers to Wage Laborers: Transformation of the Social Question*, trans. Richard Boyd, Piscataway, NJ: Transaction Publishers.

Chalvon-Demersay, Sabine (1996), 'Une société élective: scénarios pour un monde de relations choisies', *Terrain* 27: 81–100.

Chaumier, S. (2004), *L'Amour fissionne: le nouvel art d'aimer*, Paris: Fayard.

Chebel, N. (1995), *Encyclopédie de l'amour en Islam*, Paris: Payot.

(1996), *La Féminisation du monde: essai sur les Mille et Une Nuits*, Paris: Payot.

Chrétien de Troyes (1991), 'Erec and Enide', trans. Carleton W. Carroll, in *Arthurian Romances*, London: Penguin: 37–122.

Clair, I. (2008), *Les Jeunes et l'amour dans les cités*, Paris: Armand Colin.

Comte, Auguste (1851), *Politique positive*, Paris.

(1874 [1852]), *Catéchisme positiviste*, Paris.

Constable, N. (2003), *Romance on a Global Scale: Pen Pals, Virtual Ethnography and 'Mail-Order' Marriages*, Berkeley: University of California Press.

Corbin, Henri (2001), *Suhrawardi d'Alep*, Saint-Clément: Fata Morgana.

Corcuff, P. (2006), 'De l'Imaginaire utopique dans les cultures ordinaries: pistes à partir d'une enquête sur la série télévisée *Ally McBeal*', in G. Gauthier and S. Laugier, eds., *L'Ordinaire et le politique*, Paris: PUF.

Cott, Nancy (1987), *The Grounding of Modern Feminism*, New Haven: Yale University Press.

    (1996 [1992]), 'The Modern Woman of the 1920s, American Style,' in Françoise Thébaud, ed., *A History of Women in the West. V. Toward a Cultural Identity in the Twentieth Century*, Cambridge, MA: Belknap Press of Harvard University Press: 76–91.

Crouzet, M. (1965), 'Préface', in Stendhal, *De l'amour*, Paris: Garnier-Flammarion.

    (2008), *Stendhal et l'Amérique*, Paris: de Fallois.

Damasio, A. (1995), *L'Erreur de Descartes: la raison des émotions*, Paris: Odile Jacob.

Daumas, M. (1996), *La Tendresse amoureuse, XVIe – XVIIIe siècles*, Paris: Perrin.

    (2004), *Le Mariage amoureux: histoire du lien conjugal sous l'Ancien Régime*, Paris: Armand Colin.

De Giorgio, M. (1992), *Le Italiane dall'Unità a oggi*, Rome and Bari: Laterza.

Demartini, D. (2005), 'Le Discours amoureux dans le *Tristan* en prose', in B. Bedos-Reza and D. Iogna-Prat, eds., *L'Individu au Moyen Age*, Paris: Aubier.

Draelants, Hugues and Tatio Sah, Olive (2003), 'Femme camerounaise cherche mari blanc: le Net entre Eldorado et outil de reproduction', *Esprit critique* 5, 4.

Dubet, F. (2002), *Le Déclin de l'institution*, Paris: Seuil.

    (2009), *Le Travail des sociétés*, Paris: Seuil.

Duby, Georges, (1983 [1981]) *The Knight, The Lady and the Priest: The Making of Modern Marriage in Medieval France*, trans. Barbara Bray, Chicago: University of Chicago Press.

Dumont, L. (1983), *Essais sur l'individualisme*, Paris: Seuil.

Duret, P. (2007), *Le Couple face au temps*, Paris: Armand Colin.

Durkheim, Emile and Mauss, Marcel (1963 [1903]), *Primitive Classification*, trans. Rodney Needham, Chicago: University of Chicago Press.

Elias, Norbert (1969 [1939]), *The Civilizing Process*, trans. Edmund Jephcott, Oxford: Blackwell.

    (1991 [1987]), *The Society of Individuals*, trans. Edmund Jephcott, London: Continuum.

Flandrin, J.-L. (1981), *Le Sexe et l'occident: évolution des attitudes et des comportements*, Paris: Seuil.

Fourier, Charles (1941 [1808]), *Théorie des quatre mouvements et des destinées générales,* Paris: Librairie de l'Ecole Sociétaire.

(2003 [1816]), *Des Harmonies polygames en amour*, Paris: Rivages poche.

Francescato, D. (1992), *Quando l'amore finisce*, Bologna: Il Mulino.

Gauchet, Marcel (1997 [1985]) *The Disenchantment of the World: A Political History of Religion*, trans. Oscar Borge, Princeton, NJ: Princeton University Press.

(2003), *La Condition historique*, Paris: Stock.

Gaulejac, V. de (2005), *La Société malade de la gestion*, Paris: Seuil.

Geertz, Clifford (1993), 'Thick Description: Towards an Interpretive Theory of Culture', in *The Interpretation of Cultures*, London: Fontana: 3–30.

Genard, J.-L. (1995) 'Réciprocité, sexe, passion: les trois modalités de l'amour', in M. Moulin and A. Eraly, eds., *Sociologie de l'amour: variations sur le sentiment amoureux*, Brussels: Editions de l'Université de Bruxelles.

Giddens, Anthony (1992), *The Transformation of Intimacy: Love, Sexuality and Eroticism in Modern Societies*, Cambridge: Polity.

Girard, R. (2004 [1961]), *Mensonge romantique et vérité Romanesque*, Paris: Pluriel-Hachette.

Goody, J. (2006), *The Theft of History*, Cambridge: Cambridge University Press.

Grimal, P. (2002 [1988]), *L'Amour à Rome*, Paris: Payot.

Grimaldi, N. (2008), *Proust, les horreurs de l'amour*, Paris: PUF.

Gruel, L. (1991), *Pardons et châtiments: les jurés français face aux violences criminelles*, Paris: Nathan.

Guillebaud, J.-C. (1998), *La Tyrannie du plaisir*, Paris: Seuil.

Gulik, Robert van (1961), *Sexual Life in Ancient China¸* Leiden: Brill.

Heinich, N. (1991), *La Gloire de Van Gogh: essai d'anthropologie de l'admiration*, Paris: Minuit.

(1996), *Être artiste: les transformations du statut des peintres et des sculpteurs*, Paris: Klincksieck.

(2003), *Les Ambivalences de l'émancipation feminine*, Paris: Albin Michel.

Henry, M. (1993), Les Nourritures imaginaires de l'amour: le roman-photo, une mise en scène de l'amour et de la relation de couple, MA Dissertation in sociology, Université Rennes 2.

Héritier, François (1996), *Masculin/feminine: la pensée de la différence*, Paris: Odile Jacob.

Hirschman, A. (1980), *Les Passions et les interest: justifications politiques du capitalisme avant son apogée*, Paris: PUF.

(1983), *Bonheur privé, action publique*, Paris: Fayard.

Houel, Annik (1997), *Le Roman d'amour et sa lectrice: une si longue passion*, Paris: L'Harmattan.

Illouz, Eva (2007), *Cold Intimacies: The Making of Emotional Capitalism*, Cambridge: Polity.

Insel, A. (2008), 'La Part du don', in Philippe Chanial, ed., *La Société vue du don: manuel de sociologie antiutilitariste appliqué*, Paris: La Découverte.

Iogna-Prat. D. (2005), 'La Question de l'individu à l'épreuve du Moyen Âge', in B. M. Bedos-Rezak and D. Iogna-Prat, eds., *De L'Individu au Moyen Âge*', Paris: Aubier.

Jonas, H. (1963), *The Gnostic Religion: The Message of the Alien God and the Beginnings of Christianity*, Boston: Beacon Press.

Kaufmann, Jean-Claude (1995), *Corps de femmes, regards d'hommes: sociologie des seins nus*, Paris: Nathan.

(2002), *Premier Matin.: comment naît une histoire d'amour*, Paris: Armand Colin.

(2008a [1999]), *The Single Woman and the Fairy-Tale Prince*, trans. David Macey, Cambridge: Polity.

(2008b), *Quand je est un autre*, Paris: Armand Colin.

(2009 [2007]), *Gripes: The Little Quarrels of Couples*, trans. Helen Morrison, Cambridge: Polity.

(2010 [2005]), *The Meaning of Cooking*, trans. David Macey, Cambridge: Polity.

Kinsey, A. (1953), *Sexual Behaviour in the Human Female*, Philadelphia: Saunders.

Klein, E. (2008), *Galilée et les Indiens: allons-nous liquider la science?* Paris: Flammarion.

Lagrave, R.-M. (1994 [1992]), 'A Supervised Emancipation', trans. Arthur Goldhammer, in Françoise Thébaud, ed., *A History of Women in the West. V. Toward a Cultural Identity in the Twentieth Century*, Cambridge, MA: Belknap Press of Harvard University Press: 453–90.

Lambert, Y. (2007), *La Naissance des religions: de la préhistoire aux religions universalistes*, Paris: Armand Colin.

Lamchichi, A. (2006), *Femmes et islam.: l'impératif universel d'égalité*, Paris: L'Harmattan.

Lardellier, P. (2004), *Le Coeur Net.: célibat et amours sur le Web*, Paris: Belin.

Le Bart, C. (2008), *L'Individualisation*, Paris: Presses de la Fondation nationale des sciences politiques.

Le Bart, C., in collaboration with J.-C. Ambroise (2000), *Les Fans des Beatles: sociologie d'une passion*, Rennes: Presses universitaires de Rennes.

Le Gall, D. (1999), 'Amours adolescents, entre revelation et blessures intimes', *Dialogue* 146.

Lévi-Strauss, Claude (1974 [1955]), *Tristes tropiques*, trans. John Weightman and Doreen Weightman, New York: Atheneum Publishers.

Linhart, Virginie (2008), *Le Jour où mon père s'est tu*, Paris: Seuil.

Long, D. (2008), *Jésus: le rabbin qui aimait les femmes*, Paris: Bourrin.

Löwy, M. and Sayre, R. (1992), *Révolte et mélancholie: le romantisme à contre-courant de la modernité*, Paris: Payot.

Luhmann, N. (1990 [1982]), *Amour comme passion: de la codification de l'identité*, Paris: Aubier.

Lyard, F. (2008), *L'Univers des musiciens: analyse d'une expérience artistique*, Toulouse: Presses universitaires du Mirail.

Makarius, R. and Levi-Makarius, L. (1974 [1961]), *L'Origine de l'exogamie et du totémisme*, Paris: Gallimard.

Marcuse, Herbert (1955), *Eros and Civilization*, Boston: Beacon Press.

Markale, J. (1987), *L'Amour courtois, ou le couple infernal*, Paris: Imago.

Martuccelli, D. (2002), *Grammaires de l'individu* (Collection Folio-Essais), Paris: Gallimard.

(2005), *La Consistance du social: une sociologie pour la modernité*, Rennes: Presses universitaires de Rennes.

(2006), *Forgé par l'épreuve: l'individu dans la France contemporaine*, Paris: Armand Colin.

Marzona, M. (2008), *Extension du domaine de la manipulation: de l'entreprise à la vie privée*, Paris: Grasset.

Miller, D. (1998), *A Theory of Shopping*, New York: Cornell University Press.

Milton, John (1643), 'The Doctrine and Discipline of Divorce' (selections), in *Prose Writings*, introduction by M. Burton, London: Everyman's Library.

Miquel, A., ed., *Le Fou de Laylâ*, Arles: Sindbad / Actes Sud.

Montaigne, Michel de (2008 [1595]), *Essais*, Paris: Guy de Pernon.

More, Thomas (2003 [1516]), *Utopia*, trans. and with an introduction and notes by Paul Turner, London: Penguin.

Morris, C. (1972), *The Discovery of the Individual, 1050–1200*, New York: Harper & Row.

Nelli, R. (2005 [1963]), *L'Erotique des troubadours*, Toulouse: Privat.

Nemo, Philippe (2004), *Qu'-est-ce que l'Occident?* Paris: PUF.

Noizet, P. (1996), *L'Idée moderne d'amour*, Paris: Kimé.

Noyes, J. H. (1847), *The Berean*, Putney, Vermont: Office of the Spiritual Magazine.

Paz, Octavio (1995 [1994]), *The Double Flame: Love and Eroticism*, trans. Helen Lane, New York: Harcourt Brace.

Péquignot, B. (1991), *La Relation amoureuse: analyse sociologique du roman sentimental moderne*, Paris: L'Harmattan.

Pezeu-Massabuau, J. (2003), *Habiter: rêve, image, projet*, Paris: L'Harmattan.

Planhol, R. de (1921), *Les Utopistes de l'amour*, Paris: Garnier Frères.

Plato (1951 [*c*.380]), *The Symposium*, trans. W. Hamilton, Harmondsworth: Penguin.

Radway, Janice (1984), *Reading the Romance: Women, Patriarchy and Popular Literature*, Chapel Hill, NC: University of North Carolina Press.

Reich, Wilhelm (1951 [1936]), *The Sexual Revolution*, London: Vision Press.

Restif de la Bretonne (1769), *Le Pornographe, ou idées d'un honnête homme sur un projet de règlement des prostituées*, London.

Reynolds, E. (1640), *Treatise of the Passions and Faculties of the Soule of Man*, London: Robert Bostock.

Rougemont, Denis de (1983 [1940]), *Love in the Western World*, trans. Montgomery Belgion, Princeton, NJ: Princeton University Press.

Rousset, J. (1981), *Leurs Yeux se rencontrèrent: la scène de première vue dans le roman*, Paris: José Corti.

Rûzbehân, B.S. (1991), *Le Jasmin des fidèles de l'amour*, Paris: Verdier.

Sade, Donatien-Alphonse-Francis, Marquis de (2006 [1795]), *Philosophy in the Boudoir*, trans. Joachim de Neugroschel, New York: Penguin.

[1797], *La Nouvelle Justine*, Holland.

Sauvageot, A. (1994), *Voirs et savoirs, esquisse d'une sociologie du regard*, Paris: PUF.

(2003), *L'Epreuve des sens: de l'action sociale à la réalité virtuelle*, Paris: PUF.

Scholes, R. (2006), *The 'Mail-Order Bride' Industry and Its Impact on US Immigration*, on-line report available at www.uscis.gov/graphics/aboutus/resstudies/Mobappa.htm.

Schurmans, M.-N. and Dominicé, L. (1997), *Le Coup de foudre amoureux: essai de sociologie compréhensive*, Paris: PUF.

Senancour, E. (1799), *Rêveries sur la nature primitive de l'homme*, (1806), *De l'Amour*, Paris.

Serfaty-Garzon, P. (2003), *Chez soi: les territoires de l'intimité*, Paris: Armand Colin.

Shorter, Edward (1975), *The Making of the Modern Family*, New York: Basic Books.

Simmel, Georg (1898), 'On the Sociology of Religion', trans. Mark Ritter and David Frisby, in David Frisby and Mike Featherstone, eds., *Simmel on Culture*, London: Sage, 1997: 275–87.

(1984), *Georg Simmel on Women, Sexuality and Love*, trans. with an introduction by Guy Oakes, New Haven: Yale University Press.

Singly, F. de (1996), 'L'Amour et l'affection: un nouvel objet sociologique', in F. de Singly, C. Martin, A. Muxel, I. Bertaus-Wiame, M. Maruani and J. Commaille, *La Famille en questions: état de la recherche*, Paris: Syros.

(2000), *Libres ensemble: l'individualisme dans la vie commune*, Paris: Nathan.

(2005), *L'Individualisme est un humanisme*, La Tour d'Aigues: Editions de l'Aube.

Sohn, Anne-Marie (1994 [1992]), 'Between the Wars in France and England', trans. Arthur Goldhammer, in Françoise Thébaud, ed., *A History of Women in the West. V. Toward a Cultural Identity in the Twentieth Century*, Cambridge, MA: Belknap Press of Harvard University Press: 92–119.

Stendhal (1975 [1822]), *Love*, trans. Gilbert Sale and Suzanne Sale, Harmondsworth: Penguin.

Swidler, Ann (2001), *Talk of Love: How Culture Matters*, Chicago and London: University of Chicago Press.

Taylor, Charles (1989), *Sources of the Self: The Making of Modern Identity*, Cambridge: Cambridge University Press.

Teresa of Avila (1957 [1565]), *The Life of St Teresa of Avila, By Herself*, trans. with an introduction by J.M. Cohen, Harmondsworth: Penguin.

Thébaud, Françoise (1994 [1992]), 'The Great War and the Triumph of Sexual Division', trans. Arthur Goldhammer, in FrançoiseThébaud, ed., *A History of Women in the West. V. Toward a Cultural Identity in the Twentieth Century*, Cambridge, MA: Belknap Press of Harvard University Press: 21–75.

Todeschini, G. (2008 [2004]), *Richesse franciscaine: de la Pauvreté volontaire à la société de marché*, Lagrasse: Verdier.

Todorov, Tzvetan (2001 [1995]), *Life in Common: An Essay in General Anthropology*, trans. Katherine Golsen and Lucy Golsen, Lincoln, NE: University of Nebraska Press.

Urbain, J.-D. (2008), *Le Voyage était presque parfait: essai sur les voyages ratés*, Paris: Payot.

Verdon, J. (1996), *Le Plaisir au Moyen Âge*, Paris: Librairie académique Perrin.

Vernant, Jean-Pierre (1996), *L'Individu, la mort, l'amour* (Collection Folio-Histoire), Paris: Gallimard.

Wahnich, S. (2008), *La longue patience du peuple, 1792: naissance de la République*, Paris: Payot.

Walch, A. (2002), *La Spiritualité conjugale dans le catholicisme français (XVIe –XXe siècle)*, Paris: Cerf.

Wright, T. (1601), *The Passions of the Minde in Generall*, London.

Zelizer, V. (2005), *The Purchase of Intimacy*, Princeton, NJ: Princeton University Press.